At Least in

The Christians Won't Harass Me

Andrew Knight

AT LEAST IN

THE CHRISTIANS
WON'T HARASS ME

—First Edition—

Published by Knight Publications
Address correspondence, requests, and orders to:
P. O. Box 13161
Gainesville, Florida
32604-1161
www.knightpublications.com

Library of Congress Cataloging in Publication Data
Main entry under title
At Least In Hell the Christians Won't Harass Me
Catalog Card Number 98-92118

ISBN 0-9661026-3-0

Cover photo courtesy of David Blankenship

The Top Ten Christians I Hope to Avoid in Hell

10) Pesky Jehovah's Witnesses at a brisk 6:45 on Saturday morning.

9) Getting-richer-by-the-day TV evangelists with big hair, a sharp tongue, and steaming underpants.

8) Fatass Christian right talk-show hosts who tell me how to live.

7) Fatass Christian right politicians who write laws telling me how to live.

6) Cute girls who won't see me because I'm not Christian.

5) Ugly girls who keep trying to convert me.

4) Arrogant campus preachers who call students "evil masturbators" and "followers of Darwin."

3) Mean old ladies who keep sending me "Are You Sure You're Saved?" brochures.

2) Former friends who wrote me off because I'm not Christian.

1) Family members who won't have me over for fear of bringing Satan into their home.

At least in Hell the Christians won't harass me!

To the preachers at the Plaza,
who have little to learn about the Bible
but yet so much to learn.

Contents

Part IV—Appendices

Introduction

Warning: If you read the rest of this page, your mother will sell herself for grocery money and your home enema kit will embarrassingly fail in a public restroom.

Put this book down. NOW. This is not a joke. Don't let your eyes defiantly scan down the rest of the page. Close your eyes, close the book, and don't open it again. It is evil. If you read the rest of this page, terrible things will happen to you. Soon. A friend of mine read this book and last week he got the crabs. Another friend read this book and she was constipated for an entire week. They have both requested that I warn future readers.

I'm going to say this one last time. DON'T READ ANY MORE OF THIS BOOK. This is your final warning.

I guess that was a pretty preposterous warning. I mean, who'd believe it? Here's what I really meant.

Warning: If you read this book, you will spend eternity in a hot, fiery place that is full of sexual frustration, genital warts, and diarrhea. It's called Hell.

Welcome to the World of Christianity

Incoherent thoughts. Contradictory arguments. Unfounded fears. Impossible events. Fantastic stories. Exorbitant churches. Arrogant preachers. Evangelism. Power. Money. The whole package.

Christianity is a mind-controlling intoxicant whose only purpose is its own self-perpetuation. No matter how much dead "Jesus loves you," Christianity doesn't give a crap about you. It is a social entity that exists *only* because it has been able to self-replicate for the past two millennia. It is not the truth.

A brave statement, perhaps. There are no atheists in foxholes, so they say. But this is not a guess. A hope. A ploy to sell books to the millions of free-thinking non-Christians. I have no worries. Not even a tinge of fear. And when you are through with this book, neither will you.

This book is for you. It will free the Christians from the pits of Hell. It will free the doubters from the discomfort of insecurity. It will free the non-religious from the label "sinner." It will free your mind.

This book is not *really* about Christianity. This is not the Bible. If you want to read about vagrant/deity Jesus O. Nazareth or fictional accounts of events that never did or could happen, you're in the wrong aisle. If you want a history of Christianity or the effects of Baptist gospel on the menstrual cycles of lesbian rodents, check the Ph.D. thesis of a theology student.

I can't name all the apostles in order or the first line in Leviticus 3 section 12 row 8 seat 44. I don't know what God did on the eighth day or what kind of fertility pills Mary was taking, so don't ask. But when you open a book—say, the Bible—and it's opening line is "Black is white," how much further do you need to read?

They fed me their lies for twelve years. Oh, yeah. I'm a converted Christian—converted *from* Christianity. Every once in a while you'll hear of some moderately intelligent atheist-converted-Christian who makes a mint selling his *How Jesus Touched Me in All the Right Places* or *How I'm Going to Get My Piece of the American Dream by Selling This Book to a Bunch of Lonely, Gullible Old Women.* But you never hear about the Christian-born Generation X-er who shakes off Jesus like a bad case of lice. You know why? Because it's not news.

There aren't many young Christians today, and the ones who actually call themselves Christians often do so for one of these reasons: to satisfy their mothers; "just in case" (i.e. no atheists in foxholes); cultural identity (much like the Jewish faith vs. the Jewish culture); an appreciation for certain Christian principles, such as the Ten Commandments; lack of awareness of other philosophies; and association between "belief in God" and Christianity. But none of these designates Christianity.

Although Christianity includes many ideas and

stories, the most fundamental one—perhaps the test of one's belief—is, did Jesus die for your sins? In other words, will belief in him, in addition to the asking of forgiveness for those sins, lead to an eternal afterlife in Heaven, whereas a lack of belief will lead to an eternal afterlife in Hell? If the answer is no, then you are *not* a Christian, and your identification as a Christian may be confusing, deceiving, and ultimately harmful.

People are leaving Christianity like it's Cuba. And there's a reason for that. Back in the day, when the Chief couldn't explain the variations in his cannabis harvest from year to year, he invented the Weed God. But then some college punk came along, did a few hands-on studies, and took the mystery out of harvesting. Then a couple of Romans got together. One said, "The sun is a massive ball of fusing hydrogen, balancing the weight of its own gravitational attraction with the pressure due to 100-million-degree gas, around which we rotate, giving the illusion of a rising and setting sun," and the other said, "It's the Sun God, duh."

As science progresses, there is less and less mystery to be explained by the hand-waving arguments of religion. I know only a handful of Christian scientists, and their answers to simple questions are getting less and less credible. How did Moses split the sea? "Well, he didn't *actually* split the sea. It's *symbolic* for the splitting headache that results when I try to logically explain this counter-intuitive bullshit." Okay, so how did Noah fit every species on Earth on his boat? "Well, it's *symbolic*..." So what *does* the Christian scientist believe? He believes in Heaven and Hell. He *feels* God. And that's about it. And as science progresses, the beliefs of the Christian scientist will correspondingly become more vague, symbolic, and useless.

This book will provide new evidence in an attempt to rebut the few remaining arguments that the Christians possess. It will also offer a new way of looking at existence, consciousness, pleasure, pain, and the future.

This book is your protection. That is, against annoying Christians.

A Fun Philosophy

That's right. This is a fun philosophy. Forget Socrates and Aristotle. They'll put you to sleep. Take *this* book with you on your Vegas vacation to spice things up. With a Marlboro, a Bud Light, and a poolside view, it just can't be beat.

Okay, okay. I can hesitantly admit that a Clancy novel might have a little more zest than a philosophy treatise. Generally speaking, I'd rather give birth to a child through my urethra than read a philosophy book.

However, at the end of the day, all I've gotten from a Clancy novel is weary eyes and a cramped ass. A well-written philosophy book has substance. It will either directly provide answers, point you in the right direction, or at least help you ask the right questions. It will leave you with a sense of understanding and newfound clarity that neither a novel nor newspaper can provide.

Give this book a chance. It will provide new evidence and original arguments in answering some of time's most enduring questions. It will refute Christianity. And it will change how you live your life. No joke.

For example, if you believe that your death is the absolute end, would your life change by learning that there is no absolute end?

If you believe that you will go to Hell if you don't live a certain way, would your life change if you learned that Hell doesn't exist?

If you believe that you must do certain things to get into Heaven, would your life change if you learned that Heaven, too, is imaginary?

If you believe that for every up there must be a down, would you live any differently by discovering that *life is just what you make it?*

These conclusions—and more—will be derived in this book. But you must be patient. You must be attentive.

I am not naïve enough to believe that this philosophy is absolute and unchanging. This is just another addition to an ocean of possibilities. However, although I can admit that it is a theory—and little more than that—it provides new evidence and original arguments to support it. The theory is also applied to some of the most contemporary problems and discoveries, from psychology to time travel, from suicide to statistical mechanics. It may be disproven at some point in the future, and then again it may not. For this reason it must be taken seriously by the scientific and philosophical communities.

The book is written at the college undergraduate level, and can be *fully* understood by bright high school students. However, the most important explanations and applications should be comprehensible to the interested public. Most of the chapters, including the appendices, are supplemented with three or four exercise problems and solutions. The purpose of these problems is to increase your understanding of the philosophy; the content of the problems does not repeat what has already been said. If you prefer not to work the problems, simply reading the solutions may be very beneficial.

I will do my best to be simple, straightforward, clear, and interesting. However, life-changing thoughts are not always intuitive. They are not easy to come upon. They are often complex and even the world's best teachers can't simplify them.

If you're looking for a quick-fix, you're in the wrong aisle. Look up Anthony Robbins for a life fix or John Gray for a relationship fix. They'll spit it out word by word, so that even a mentally challenged second-grader won't have any trouble following it.

This is not a quick-fix. This is a philosophy that will touch on some of the most passionate and popular contemporary questions. It will intrigue you. It will inspire you. And it will free you.

This is a fun philosophy.

The Origin of This Philosophy

The thing I first learned is that I exist. I learned this long before I heard or read about Descartes' *cogito ergo sum*[1]. When it first hit me, I so "clearly and distinctly perceived" it, to use Descartes' tongue, that in comparison I knew nothing else. I exist independently of anything: a God, an external world, love, sustenance.

[1] I think, therefore I am.

That was eighth grade.

Lots of philosophers have tried to show that we can know things through our perceptions. For example, God is not a deceiver, so what we sense is true. Or, there are things which we can perceive which we cannot perfectly recreate in our minds, so external things exist, and stimulate our senses accordingly. I'm still not convinced. But there *are* some things I can know which depend only on the knowledge that I exist.

In ninth grade, I dismissed Christmas for the first time as a sensationalized commercial holiday in which the rich got richer and the poor tried desperately to atone for their unforgivable sins by giving overpriced presents. I guess it was around the same time that I admitted to myself that there was little or no evidence to support the lessons I learned in church. Some evidence was even counterproductive, in that it made me less likely to believe the hocus-pocus stories of the Old Testament. Even if Moses could part the sea, the bottom of the ocean isn't exactly a paved sidewalk. And what if the two zebras on Noah's ark weren't sexually attracted to each other? Then what?

Clearly, this admission was a dangerous one. If Jesus of Nazareth was, in fact, the graven image we should all worship, then wouldn't God damn us to an eternity of fire, brimstone, and *Beverly Hills 90210* if we didn't? It frightened me to think that if I didn't believe every word in the Bible and every sentence from my preacher's mouth, I would feel pain. Forever. So even though I had never fully bought Christianity, I came to terms with my absence of faith only when it occurred to me that God, the omnipotent creator, had meant for me to be smart and inquisitive, had meant for me to receive all the influences I had, and had therefore meant for me to doubt Christianity. How could he punish me for something that I was destined to do, and therefore had no control over?[2]

Some people justify their faith on the same scare tactics that most Christians and I today have experienced: does it really hurt a person to mindlessly believe a fairy tale "just in case?" Yes!—because it excludes the possibility of ever learning the truth. And since the only sensible mission in life I can think of is learning, such an act would thwart my mission.

"You're not Christian?" some ask. "Don't you believe in god?" *God* does not imply Christianity. Lots of religions subscribe to the thought of a higher being. Christianity is a very specific set of memes[3] which have been successful in spreading for the past couple of millennia. I suppose it would include stories about a vagrant named Jesus and mutually exclusive concepts like *God loves all* and *God damns pro-choicers.* I did not necessarily give up the concepts of god, love, and ethics by repudiating Christianity.

---

[2]The fate vs. free will argument will be discussed later. Even though I do not presently subscribe to a belief in fate, it is exactly this belief that originally gave me the confidence to doubt Christianity.

[3]Memes are cultural genes which are subject to the same haphazard natural selection that occurs in biological evolution. An excellent source of information on the subject of cultural evolution is *Virus of the Mind* by Richard Brodie.

Around the same time, I was confronted with some basic calculus-like contradictions. Stuff like infinity squared and one divided by zero. After developing a theory of my own, I wrote *Knight's Null Algebra*[4]. In doing so, I remember lying awake night after night, hours upon hours, thinking. What's beyond infinity? Does infinity exist in the physical world? Does infinity exist in time?

I can't put my finger on the day exactly, or even the month, but I remember when my eternal existence first occurred to me. My eyes were closed, not a sound. But an active mind, spinning endlessly. Suddenly my consciousness became rock solid. No body, no senses. Just memories and an awareness of self. It quickly occurred to me that only two mutually exclusive possibilities existed: either my consciousness would end, or it wouldn't. Sort of like the poster I once read: "Either we are alone in the universe or we are not. Both ideas are overwhelming." Either I will cease to exist or I won't. A pretty obvious statement, but with frightful implications.

My brain wouldn't slow down. I quickly realized that if at some point in the future my consciousness were to end, I couldn't be conscious right now, because I would not be able to recall being conscious[5]. As clearly and distinctly as Descartes perceived his own existence and its eternal nature, I knew that my consciousness could not possibly end.

I remember breathing hard and quick. The pounding of my heart interrupted my thoughts. I got out

---

[4]ISBN 0-9661026-1-4

[5]This will be shown in *Is There an Afterlife?*

of bed and paced fast circles in my room in the dark. But it didn't help. I paced to the living room, turned on the light and the radio, and paced some more. I finally fell asleep with the radio blasting away my thoughts.

It's happened over twenty times since that first night. It's hell. It's the ultimate fear because it's the one that I can't escape, no matter what I do. On the occasional night that I feel particularly aware, I lie awake thinking. Somehow my thoughts almost always wander to my future, and the *creature* comes back. Yep. It still happens. But as a product of evolution, I've gotten pretty good at preventing it. As soon as my thoughts enter the realm of eternity, I turn on the radio. I've succeeded in preventing the *creature* a good two dozen times in the past.

But it will happen again. It will happen infinitely[6]. I will forever be reminded that my existence is eternal. I will forever be reminded that I can't give up. I can't go bankrupt. I can't fold. I'm in this for good. I can't turn around. I can't cease to exist even if I so desired. It will always scare me to death but I'll never die[7].

Structure of This Book

The purpose of this book is to provide a new, clear, and rational approach to some of time's most enduring theological and philosophical questions. All of these questions can more or less be answered in the Bible,

---

[6]This will also be shown in *Is There an Afterlife?*
[7]Figuratively speaking

so my first goal is to repudiate the Bible by discrediting Christianity as a whole. I will do this by presenting some of the fundamental problems with Christianity, and how these problems are detrimental to individuals, society, and free thought in general. My second goal will be the presentation of a new point of view, based on new evidence and original proofs. This new point of view, if correct, will answer such questions as, "Is there an afterlife?" "Is there a Heaven or Hell?" and "Is there a god?" My third goal will be the presentation of a mathematical model which will help answer and clarify questions like, "Are there pleasure and pain debts?" "How much pleasure and pain will I experience?" and "What is the key to happiness?"

In satisfying all three goals, I will constantly present applications of the arguments. For example, I will provide examples of how society would be better without Christianity. As another example, I will provide examples of how one can improve the quality of her life by applying the model to it.

Thank you for reading this book. I hope to stimulate you intellectually, offer new possibilities, and enrich your life with a deeper understanding of existence.

Part I

Christianity

What Are the Detriments of Christianity?

What Are the Detriments of Christianity?

This chapter will identify many fundamental detriments of Christianity and provide solutions, where appropriate. It will show that the ability of Christianity to survive and spread relies on the very aspects that make it detrimental.

The Plaza Preachers

The Plaza Preachers are going to Hell. Everyone agrees.

There's a spot at the University of Florida—a beautiful lawn with wide oaks and shaded benches—where students come to read, smoke, talk, and sleep. It's in front of the library, and about three days of the week one can watch the jugglers practice and listen to the music majors strum a guitar. The Hare Krishnas offer vegetarian lunches for a $1 donation and the background sound of their drums is relaxing, rhythmic like one's heartbeat. It's a place to unwind.

That is, until the Preachers show up.

A group of three or four area Christian preachers, dressed in dark orange sport jackets, interrupt the serenity at least twice a week. They stand in the middle of the Plaza and, one at a time, yell at the students. A preacher holds his Bible to the right side of his mouth and, in monotone, speaks common, catchy phrases about Jesus. "Jesus is our lord, our salvation. The only way to Heaven is through Jesus; the only method of salvation is to let Jesus into your heart." He then pauses for a moment, appearing to search for his next statement, and then he shuffles his words around a little. "Jesus is Lord. To know Jesus is to know love, and to know love is to know Heaven. Only Jesus can save you." The content of the lecture is narrow and unoriginal, though loud. When the preacher finally recognizes that his message is not being heeded, or perhaps when he becomes self-conscious of the circular nature of his lecture, he becomes more aggressive.

He points his finger at a student who is dressed in tight jeans and a tight shirt and calls her a whore. "This woman is infiltrated with Satan. She is living in sin by her tempting dress and her whorish ways. This woman does not know God and will spend all eternity in Hell unless she asks God for forgiveness and surrenders her life to Jesus." The girl just walks away.

Then the preacher points at a student reading. "This man is a sinner. He is reading, yes, but it is not the Bible. This man does not know God." The man looks up, his eyebrows slanted in annoyance.

"I'm studying for class. Is that a problem? Am I going to Hell for trying to *learn*?"

"Yes!" shouts the Preacher, excited to get a response. "You need to put that book away. It is confusing you. It is leading you in the wrong direction. The scientists don't know the answers. The researchers and professors don't know the answers. An open mind is open to Satan. Focus on the truth and close your mind to everything else. Read the Bible. Study the Bible." The student shakes his head and looks back down at his book. But the Preacher isn't finished. He walks to the student, reaches into his hands, and closes the book with a loud clap. The student jumps up, enraged, and pushes him away.

"Get the fuck away from me!" he shouts as tears welt up in his eyes. He grabs his books and walks away frantically.

Then the Preacher points at a student in a group. The student is pierced in his ears, nose, and bottom lip; his hair is purple. "Look at this freak. Freaks don't get into Heaven. Remove those evil rings and focus on what is right and true. Be conservative." The student turns to his friends and chuckles. The Preacher continues. "Oh, is that funny? I bet you're a masturbator, too. You masturbate, don't you?" At this, a general laughter rises in the crowd.

The student stands up. "No, I don't need to masturbate. I got your momma." He and his friends laugh.

Masturbation appears to have hit the spot. The next three hours he preaches nonstop on the same subject. After calling ten students "evil masturbators," he finally concludes that the only way to escape masturbation—and to enter the kingdom of Heaven—is through "our Lord, Jesus Christ."

Challenging the Plaza Preachers

Are the Plaza Preachers taken seriously? Do they successfully convert nonbelievers to Christianity? It is doubtful.

In the Plaza, the Preachers rarely generate an audience. They simply take advantage of an already populated area to preach. It is unreasonable to imagine that many of these students choose to sit at the Plaza for the *purpose* of listening to the Preachers. When the Preachers do generate a crowd, it is by offending and insulting passers-by.

There is a second common preaching location on campus. Here, a self-made audience of ten to twenty people occasionally evolves. Of this audience, I estimate, and the Preachers even admit, that "approximately 85% of the listeners are nonbelievers and listen only for entertainment."

Clearly, with this kind of resistance, it is not surprising that the Preachers are often challenged.

"When the Bible appears to contradict itself over important facts—e.g. the creation of the heavens—should it not be discredited as an historical text?" one student asks.

The Preacher responds, "There are no contradictions in the Bible. The Bible was inspired by God, who does not make mistakes."

"I am aware that the Bible claims Creation something like six thousand years ago. How might one explain carbon dating, which dates objects to fifty thousand years? Or what about natural radioisotope dating, which dates the earth at 4.6 billion years, or Doppler shift dating, which dates the Universe at fifteen billion years, or any number of other dating methods, none of which lend credence to the claims in the Bible?"

"Science deceives. Nothing is as sure as the Bible. If it is true that the moon was formed four billion years ago, then when we first visited the moon in 1969, we should have expected a four-foot-thick layer of unpacked moon dust that never settled, due to the lack of an atmosphere on the moon. But when we landed, the layer of dust was only a few inches deep, which means that the moon was created recently, not four billion years ago."

"I've never heard of that experiment."

"There are lots of experiments that you haven't heard of, because you've only been taught by heathens and atheists."

"Well, how might one explain the existence of dinosaurs, which are dated at millions of years ago?"

"The dinosaurs coincided with humans," the Preacher responds.

"Would the dinosaurs have been included on Noah's Ark, then?" The Preacher nods. The student continues. "Are you familiar with the number of species in existence?" Another nod. "Is it then conceivable that two of every animal fit on Noah's Ark, including the dinosaurs?"

"The Ark was about as big as a football stadium. Lots of animals could fit on it."

"I am aware of the Bible's claim that every living thing died during that flooding, so all of today's creatures resulted from only a male and female of each species. Are you familiar with the statistical abnormalities and dangers that result from inbreeding?"

"Yes. After inbreeding for a long period of time, the resulting animals might become mean, sometimes angry."

"So is it safe to say that the children of a brother and sister will be fine; and only the offspring of their offspring will feel the effects, which are 'to become mean'?" The Plaza Preacher doesn't answer. "And what about us? Didn't we all come from Adam and Eve? So did their children's inbreeding make us all mean?" The Plaza Preacher ignores the response and answers another student's question.

"Is it possible for a species to adapt to its environment?" The Preacher looks thoughtful, and then nods. "If so, then is it not conceivable for a species of fish, in adapting to a drying environment, to breathe air and walk on land with its fins?"

The debate goes on and on and on. They discuss the age of the universe, the parting of the Red Sea by Moses, the feeding of thousands of people with a single basket of food, resurrection, walking on water, and Adam and Eve. The Preacher's arguments are often lacking in validity, and his logic usually circular. When it is clear that the evidence is insurmountable against a particular claim in the Bible, he claims, "Let's not dote on that aspect too much. You're getting away from the big picture, that Jesus Christ is the path to salvation. Not everything in the Bible can be explained yet, but lots of things haven't been explained yet."

Ultimately, the Preachers spend most of their lectures on easily understandable, attention-getting, and readily spreading phrases like, "We are all sinners," "Sinners will go to Hell," "Jesus can forgive our sins," "Those forgiven will go to Heaven," "Heaven is a beautiful place where we are one with God," and "Hell is eternal fire, torture, and pain."

The Plaza Preachers do not represent all Christians, and some would argue that they are terrible spokesmen for Christianity. However, what is not in debate is that the Plaza Preachers represent the worst aspects of Christianity.

Detriments of Christianity

All too often I hear the claim, "Life with Jesus is a win-win situation. What have you got to lose? And if you're right, then you will get into Heaven and avoid Hell."

Ironically, the truth is that Christianity is a *lose-lose* situation. This book will attempt to show, through logic and mathematics, that no such entity as Heaven or Hell can exist. In that regard, Christianity is a loss, because it drives people to preclude many potentially pleasurable experiences from their lives in attempting to avoid Hell, and to spend a great deal of time pursuing useless or painful activities in attempting to get into Heaven. Examples of such activities will be given later. However, the evidence I will present for the nonexistence of Heaven and Hell is controversial in the philosophical community (to say the least), so let me comment on the second "loss" in the lose-lose situation in Christianity.

Irregardless of what happens in the afterlife (if there is one), Christianity harms people *now*, in three fundamental ways.

First, Evangelism

Christianity is a social entity, much like a corporation or an organization. It isn't a *thing*, really, but a concept that exists only in human minds. Not many people would disagree with the statement that, lacking human minds, social entities—including Christianity—would not exist. An entity, living or not, is subject to the same haphazard natural selection that we observe in the evolution of species. At its most basic level, evolution is best described by, "It will be here tomorrow only if it can survive and reproduce today."

Christianity is here today because it has been able to survive and reproduce (spread) for the past two millennia. That is the ONLY reason. Even though this statement is difficult to rebut, some intelligent Christians will then claim, "Christianity has been able to survive and reproduce for the past two millennia because it is the *truth*." Unfortunately, truth does not necessarily spread the best. Only what is attractive, or scary, or comforting, or alarming spreads. If the truth is attractive, or scary, or comforting, or alarming, then it will spread. But if the truth is dull, or unintuitive, people don't generally talk about it, and so it doesn't quickly spread among the masses.

The heliocentric view of the universe, first proposed by Galileo, was not comforting to the masses at the time of its proposal. People wanted to believe that human consciousness was at the heart of the universe, and the idea that we rotated about the sun—rather than the heavens revolving around us—was unsettling. We know the truth today, but only after coming upon the realization that the most intuitive or likeable answer is not always the correct one. Ironically, intuition *rarely* points at a correct answer.

What spreads and what does not is hard to predict. Social scientists concerned with memology—or the study of the evolution of human ideas—have provided some information as to the "spreadability" of an idea. It is largely based on the instinctual cues that all humans and animals are born with. For example, restaurant commercials that make us *hungry* are successful. A radon gas detector commercial that *scares* us is successful. A Sally Struthers save-the-children commercial that plays on our *sympathy* is successful. A movie preview that is sexually *exciting* is successful. Richard Brodie in *The Virus of the Mind* names the four f's of successful memes: those that play on our instinctual desire for fighting, fleeing, feeding, and—well, reproducing.

Christianity successfully plays on these desires. It scares us with Hell and entices us with Heaven. That is certainly one reason that Christianity has been able to survive and spread through the ages.

One basic principle of Christianity is that of evangelism. Christians, who are the agents of the social entity Christianity, must spread the beliefs, or else the entity will die. Members of the church of Jehovah's Witnesses are notorious for showing up on middle-class doorsteps at seven or eight on Saturday mornings to "teach" their views—or, more correctly, to solicit membership to their church. Most denominations advocate missions, on which church youth travel throughout the country—often at their own expense—to convert people to their religion. Television evangelists, if crafty and persuasive enough, are able to keep small groups of people funding the conversion efforts of the entire television program. Certainly within each church is the constant suggestion to bring friends and colleagues, and churches continue to advertise as would any business.

Christianity must do these things to survive. It must be evangelistic. And that, in itself, doesn't appear detrimental. After all, a car company must advertise, and the company that has the best advertisements and easiest spreading memes will sell the most cars.

But a car company can't sell a rock and call it a car. There are certain minimum requirements a car must meet before it even becomes subject to the natural selection of its memes. For example, it must have an engine that works. It must have wheels. It should not break down every fifth mile. It should be designed so that it doesn't burst into flames upon reaching 60 miles per hour. These are a few among many minimum standards. Once a car is a car, and it is reliable, then it doesn't seem to matter whether a *blue* car is more popular (spreads better) than a *green* car—they are both sufficient to be labeled as cars. It doesn't really matter if the left-side steering wheel is more liked than the right-side steering wheel. Evolution of this sort doesn't change the *essence* of the car.

However, in the case of Christianity, or any religion, the "product" is truth. Or, rather, the product is a collection of stories and concepts that are packaged and sold as truth[1]. And whether a statement has the minimum requirement of *truth* is not as cut-and-dry as the minimum requirements of a car. After all, if you get into a car and it doesn't take you anywhere, then it would seem reasonable to complain to the manufacturer. *Anybody* would do that much. But when a Christian claims, "Jesus is Lord," it is not quite so straightforward to respond, "Jesus is *not* lord." It appears to be more debatable. And it is this gray that has allowed Christianity to survive well into the most enlightened, investigative, and free-thinking age in human history.

The detriment of Christianity's evangelism is simply this. Christianity has spread, but only because it possesses ideas that spread easily. The ideas that spread easily are not necessarily those that are most true. The evangelistic nature of Christianity is neither a search for nor a spreading of truth, but rather a self-perpetuation of an entity whose sole purpose is self-perpetuation. So even if Christianity ever did possess the essence of truth, it has long since been distorted by what is most interesting, or scary, or intuitive.

---

[1]Just imagine "lowfat truth" and "caffeine-free truth!" If someone could find a way to successfully market them, you'd better believe he would.

The attribution of "truth" to Christianity is analogous to the attribution of truth to the movie, *Star Wars*; both are popular self-perpetuating entities, and that's all. It is time for Christians to recognize that Christianity is not "inspired;" it is a man-made invention that, much like the Bee Gees, is trying desperately to *stay alive*.

Second, Exclusivity

Christianity, as an entity, is only concerned[2] with its own self-perpetuation. Contrary to popular view, a Christian is no better or "moral" than a non-Christian. It is an appearance only.

It *appears* as if Christians are good, decent, moral people, but in fact the opposite is often true. Christianity needs people, and its "weed-out" process is not as stringent as one might expect. In fact, this exclusivity has nothing to do with the background, ethics, or morals of those that it attempts to convert. Convicted murderers, thieves, and rapists are prime prospects for Christianity. Alcoholics and crack addicts are welcomed with open

---

[2]Christianity is not a conscious thing, so it can't very well be "concerned" about anything. Similarly, a virus, which scientists aren't even convinced is a living being, is concerned only with its own replication. What I actually mean is that, because the virus has survived many generations, it is likely that in its chemical and physical activities, it will pursue further replication. Similarly, Christianity, which has survived two millennia, is likely to possess attributes that will result in its spreading.

arms. Child molesters, wife beaters, and adulteresses become brothers and sisters just as soon as they proclaim faith in Jesus. Liars, cheaters, bullies, and regular assholes are the staple of Christianity.

This is the rule, *not* the exception. Ironically, it is the murderers, alcoholics, and child molesters who are most easily converted; therefore, the strongest efforts to perpetuate Christianity are in them.

All too often, one hears about a former heroine addict or prostitute who was "saved" by Jesus. However, what was the context of this alleged event? You will probably find that the prostitute was at the end of her ropes, at rock bottom. She was sick, penniless, homeless, and completely rejected by those she trusted. It seems likely that *any* philosophy that resulted in a more pleasurable way of life would have appeared to "save" her at that point. It just so happens that a Bible pusher walked in her life right at that moment.

Christianity preys on the tired, helpless, and hopeless like a vulture on roadkill. Even decent, respectable people lose hope and initiative occasionally. A woman who was sexually abused as a child is not responsible for her abuse, but she may suffer psychological problems due to this abuse. If she cannot find reasonable strength within herself, or she is searching for an explanation that may not exist, she may fall to the downy comforts of Christianity.

Christians who have had a "normal" childhood (lacking psychological or physical abuse) and have established a comfortable niche in society often find themselves asking, "What is Christianity doing for me?"

Christianity needs people to continue its self-replication. It is open to anyone who is open to it. Ultimately, however, the best prospects and strongest self-perpetuators are the weak, abused, rejected, and irresponsible.

It *appears* as if Christianity is inclusive and accepting of all, but in fact the opposite it true. *Christianity violently excludes anyone who will not convert.* As long as a person appears open to the possibility of Christianity, Christians will flock to that person in a façade of love, acceptance, and forgiveness. However, the moment that the person shakes his head no, "I don't believe that Jesus is the son of God and I don't believe that I am a sinner," Christians will damn that person to an eternity of fire and brimstone[3]. It is not ethics or morals that is the basis of exclusivity in Christianity, but rather one's *potential* for becoming a Christian.

What are the implications of this exclusion? Is the result a simple "agreement to disagree?" Absolutely not. Rather, it is all-out ostracism, oppression, and, in the case of religious wars, genocide.

First, Christians will avoid befriending non-Christians[4]. Then, upon discovering that a certain friend

---

[3]Christians claim that only god can damn. However, it is ultimately the Christians who have taken upon the responsibility of relaying this arrogant and cruel command.

[4]I use "non-Christian" to mean non-convertible—i.e. someone who has excluded any possibility of Christianity.

is not a Christian and will never be a Christian, they will alienate that friend. This is also true of family members; how many family relationships have been irreparably severed for differences in religious views? No other subject disagreement—whether it be as trivial as football or as weighty as politics—comes close to the damage done by religion.

The oppression comes in a variety of forms. A qualified candidate may be refused a job because he refuses to accept the Christian beliefs or lifestyle. A non-Christian on trial may be judged unfairly by a Christian jury. A public figure may be defamed or discredited because he is labeled "evil" or "Satanic" or "atheist[5]." A citizen may be ruled by Christian values that infringe on his rights. Examples of this include institutionalized marriage, laws prohibiting certain sex acts or nudity, laws promoting prayer, and laws concerning gambling, prostitution, drug use, and euthanasia[6] when written in a "moral" context.

Christians are able to sleep at night because they justify their actions. By assigning the label "bad," "sinner," or "immoral" to non-Christians, Christians avoid

---

Also, I use "Christian" to mean devout Christian, not one who is only socially Christian.

[5]Non-Christian is not equivalent to "atheist." *Non-Christian* means not subscribing to the concepts, stories, and beliefs that comprise Christianity, where *atheist* means believing that a god does not exist *or* not subscribing to any religious beliefs. "Atheist" is often perceived negatively in a Christian society.

[6]Some of the so-called victimless crimes.

them for the same reasons that any rational person might want to avoid a serial killer or a kleptomaniac. Then they assign the label "bad influence" to the non-Christian and urge their friends, family, and children to avoid them, too. Christians believe that it is their god-given right to pass judgement on, mistreat, ignore, or violate the rights of non-Christians.

There are too many decent, respectable, ethical non-Christians in this world to let this myth be perpetuated any longer.

Everyone loses from this exclusivity. Ultimately, friendships and family bonds are prevented or broken because of the existence of a mental entity whose only goal is self-replication.

Third, Ignorance

One of the Plaza Preachers talked about a narrow path. "Once you know Jesus, and have accepted him, all the misunderstandings and so-called discrepancies [in the Bible] become subordinate. You live on a narrow path and have faith in the answers we have been given. An open mind is open to Satan. A narrow mind is one with God."

"That's exactly the problem with Christianity," a student answered.

I agree. Needless to say, the Preacher's comments did not fare well with the minorities in the audience. After all, only an open mind is capable of treating each person (or situation) as an individual; an narrow mind sees the world in a fixed, unchanging way, and bases his judgements on past information that may no longer be valid. A narrow mind is a prejudiced mind.

Not only does this position present clear problems in the day-to-day life of contemporary society, but it distorts the holder's view of reality, a detriment to the holder. Say, for example, a tiger is chasing Bob, who is a devout believer in Schmistianity. Bob reads a short verse from the Schmible, "Thou shalt be saved from hungry tigers if thou believeth in me." Instead of running, Bob prays to Schmod. Finally, Bob gets a good taste of reality when the tiger gets a good taste of him.

Christians in the Middle Ages firmly subscribed to the belief in a flat Earth. Regardless of reasonable evidence to the contrary, uncountable Christians died ignorant, deceived by their Bible. "The earth is flat; that is the absolute truth. There is no getting around it. You cannot possibly prove that the earth is round because it is not. That Columbus guy is a freak."

How many times have you heard a Christian swear up and down to his beliefs, without providing any evidence other than "faith?" They, too, will die with a firm conviction in many falsities, whose truth either may come in the future or already exists.

Ignorant can mean *uneducated* or *ignoring*. Christians are often unaware of the evidence that may discredit their Bible, or else they ignore it. However, it is inconceivable that most Christians are unaware of this evidence because they don't know it exists. Rather, they generally know that it exists, and *choose* to remain unaware.

Here's the problem with being ignorant—i.e. "narrow-minded" as the Preacher put it. No matter how much evidence one has collected in showing something, or the nature of that evidence, or the weight of that evidence, Christianity ignores it. Take, for example, the Christian claim that an afterlife exists. A devout narrow-minded Christian will believe this irregardless of the evidence. She will ostracise non-Christians. She will ignore any evidence to the contrary. She will defend her belief until the day she dies. Wouldn't it be ironic if, the moment she died, nothing more happened? If her brain and consciousness just ceased to function? If she found herself in neither Heaven nor Hell? *If she did not find herself at all?* What then? Would it finally be reasonable to state that an afterlife does not exist? Would *that* be enough evidence?

Most Christians would answer in the positive. However, on the same token, many Christians swear up and down that the world is six thousand years old, an issue that has been settled long ago. That's right—this issue has been settled long, long ago. The evidence for a very old universe in insurmountable. It *is* conceivable that every experiment ever done regarding the age of the universe is invalid and the results incorrect, though very (*very*) unlikely. However, other than the Bible, there is little evidence (particularly scientific) of a young universe. My question is this: how much more evidence do the Christians need? Much like the analogy of the dead Christian who never finds an afterlife, what kind of indisputable evidence will be required to change the Christian's mind? If the Christian is, in fact, narrow-minded to the teachings of the Bible, then NO amount of evidence will change his mind.

Narrow-mindedness is irrationality. I do not want as a jury a group of people who believes in good faith that Abraham was justified in killing his son. I do not want a professor teaching me physics who is convinced that Moses parted the Red Sea. I do not want a spouse arguing with me about finances who believes that Jesus fed ten-thousand people with a picnic basket of food. I do not want a politician leading an army who has been sent from god to destroy all infidels.

One who has closed his mind to other possibilities has stopped learning. Staying open-minded is not only the politically correct thing to do, it is ultimately beneficial. An open-minded person will be able to avoid pain and pursue pleasure using information that was previously unavailable; he is also more adaptable to his surroundings.

The Price is Right—*Christian Right*

What I've mentioned are the three fundamental problems that keep Christians on their "narrow path" of irrationality and ignorance. There are many other detriments to consider, however. Try economics.

A business doesn't stop paying rent when its doors close. But the business may stop paying its employees when the lights go out. So, the operation of a business is always concerned with the proper balance between transacted business when the doors are open and lost business when the doors are closed.

Ultimately, the consumer pays all the business expenses of all successful businesses in operation. When you shop at the mall, you are indirectly paying for the rent of the mall while it is both open and closed. However, this financial burden is distributed over enough customers during open hours that the cost of products from the mall is reasonable (according to my girlfriend).

How much time during the week is the average church conducting business? A single day! But not even the entire day. Usually, the church sermon lasts an hour, and the congregation socializes for another hour. So, the church is conducting business for two out of the 168 hours in a week, which is less than 2% of its potential. This translates into a church "rent" that is 84 times as high as it should be, if the church were used 24 hours a day. While many churches are large, extravagant, expensive buildings, *all* churches are paid for by their congregation, which only uses the church for a few hours a week.

Some churches provide a Wednesday Bible study class or the like, but the small groups that attend hardly require the space or contents of an entire church. For the rest of the time, churches lie dormant. Considering the number of homeless citizens across the country, it is a shame that so much space, capital, and potential productivity is wasted on a quiet, empty church. All in all, churches are a horrible financial investment, particularly on the part of the congregation.

Christianity vs. the Lottery

Which is the better deal? I think I'd bet the Lottery.

Christianity makes promises it can't keep. It's that simple. It instills false hopes in its followers for a hefty price. It offers an alternate, distorted view of reality; again, nothing is free, particularly Christianity.

The argument will be made that the Bible is completely correct and therefore my statement that "Christianity makes promises it can't keep" is both a personal opinion as well as an *incorrect* personal opinion. And that may or may not be true. However, the Bible is simply the physical product of Christianity; the stories and concepts in it is not Christianity, per se. Rather, Christianity consists of the stories and concepts that spread the best, as noted in the previous section on evangelism. Consider.

How many interpretations exist of Heisenberg's Uncertainty Principle or Einstein's General Theory of Relativity? Not many. The number *one* comes to mind. How many interpretations exist of Noah's Ark? I don't think I have enough fingers to count.

Some state that two of every creature on Earth were on the Ark, and all others died in the flood. Others state that it was only two of every bird and beast. Still others state that only a small region was flooded, not the entire world. Some say that the flood lasted half a year, while others say that it lasted forty days and nights. Some even claim that the story is completely symbolic. These are only a handful of the interpretations that I have heard firsthand from friends and acquaintances claiming to be Christian. Whether or not any of the interpretations is valid, founded, or even rational is irrelevant. The point is that there are Christians in the world who would firmly clutch to each of the above interpretations, and probably a thousand others.

There are a thousand interpretations for each of a thousand stories or concepts in the Bible, and many Christian denominations endorsing specific sets of interpretations. Unfortunately, if the Bible is correct (which is doubtful), only one interpretation of each of the stories is correct. Let me say that again. At most, only one interpretation of each of the stories is correct. For example, it is impossible for Adam and Eve to have been the first humans alive and simultaneously for cities to have existed while they were alive. In other words, different Christian denominations and preachers sell different versions of the "truth," the most of which only one can be true.

This situation is analogous even to "universal" Christian concepts like Heaven and Hell. Some Christians are taught that people enter Heaven or Hell immediately after dying, while others are taught that they will enter a "state of limbo" called Purgatory. Some are taught that Purgatory will end on Judgment Day, in which case they will enter Heaven or Hell, and others are taught that there are varying "levels" of Heaven and Hell. Some are taught that God judges them based on the number of sins they have committed in life, while others are taught that they are judged based on whether or not they have repented for their sins. One of my favorite questions to Christians is this: "If a Christian man rapes a girl under the pretense that he will later ask for forgiveness, can he still get into Heaven?" Not surprisingly, the answers I receive vary considerably.

Here's my point: even if there is a Heaven and Hell—again, which is doubtful—Christian preachers make so many conflicting promises that, at most, only a small percentage can actually be "kept." In other words, Christianity isn't selling the truth; rather, it is selling a *probability* of truth.

How is this different from gambling in the lottery? If I sell you a lottery ticket and *promise* that you will win, did I "keep" my promise if you actually do win? Of course not. It was the luck of the draw. No Christian can reasonably make *any* promise regarding her views, because it is not within her power to fulfill that promise; either she is right or she is not.

Christianity is no different from the lottery, other than that your chances are better in the lottery. Both are in the business of selling chances; one offers a chance at ten million dollars, and the other offers a chance at eternal salvation. Unfortunately, your odds of "winning" in either case is practically zero. So, instead of viewing your preacher as a holy, inspired professor, maybe he is better viewed as a midnight-shift 7-11 attendant trying desperately to sell you a lottery ticket. Either way, you are ultimately being deceived by those who've got their eyes on your money.

A Distorted View of Reality

Think of the worst relationship you've ever had. Maybe she cheated on you. Maybe he physically abused you. When the relationship was finally over, did you say to yourself, "He'll get what he deserves," or "God knows what she did and she'll be punished?" It made you feel better, didn't it? The thought that there is some omnipotent judge that rights all wrongs is very comforting. It makes life less stressful—temporarily.

After all, it *could* be true that the following week your ex is jailed for solicitation. Unfortunately, it is also just as likely that your ex finds a beautiful wife, makes partner at a prestigious law firm, and buys a brand new Ferrari.

Christianity offers hope when hope doesn't necessarily exist. In that sense, it provides a distorted view of reality. After all, a Christian might spend his entire life preparing for a life in Heaven, even though it is perfectly conceivable that Heaven does not exist. How will that Christian feel then? A little let-down? A little deceived? A little resentful of Christianity?

Consider. If I promised you that tomorrow you would have the best sex of your life, and you were *convinced* that tomorrow you would have the best sex of your life, then you would probably feel pretty good today. The thought would be exciting, and fulfilling, and it would allow you to take today's troubles with a grain of salt. I instilled in you a false hope. But what happens when tomorrow comes and the prophecy turned out to be a lie? All of the pleasure you garnished from today's hopes would turn into pain garnished from tomorrow's frustration. The same is true of Christianity.

The price you pay for the hopes offered by Christianity today is the confusion and pain you will feel when you discover that Christianity is incorrect.

I've heard the argument that it doesn't hurt to believe Christianity, even if Christianity offers false hopes. After all, think of all the hospital patients and accident victims who have recovered due to their faith and hope in Jesus. My response: think of all the hopeless, scared teenagers who have killed themselves in hope of a better life in Heaven.

This book will attempt to show that life after death is not significantly different from life, in terms of pleasure and pain. If I am successful in convincing a young, suicidal girl of this philosophy, then I may be able to convince her that the *only* way to end her pain is to deal with her problems. If I can do that, then I will save that young girl's life, and make her stronger and more independent in the meanwhile.

Every suicide caused by the hope of a better life in Heaven is a homicide perpetrated by Christians.

Christian Resistance

Of particular annoyance to Christians is my frustrating determination to solve my own problems and assume responsibility for my own actions. Completely disregarding the simple problems with Christianity—say, for example, the fact that humans can't walk on water—I will never be converted to Christianity because I don't need an omnipotent being to give me the answers to my problems. I don't need a fallen angel on which to blame my shortcomings. I wasn't molested as a child and I never had to live on the streets. I didn't grow up in a detention home and I've never been left for dead. I've had my share of challenges, but, with the help of my family, friends, and a clear, rational mind, I overcame them. I didn't need Jesus to be my friend and I didn't need Satan to be my enemy. I don't need Christianity, and that seriously bothers Christians.

Christianity relies on powerful emotions to suppress the logical part of the brain that screams, "What the hell is this? This doesn't make any sense!"

Again, these emotions are often very powerful in criminal offenders, victims of horrible (particularly sexual) crimes, alcohol and drug addicts, war survivors, and anyone who has witnessed something awful—e.g. an eight-year-old witnessing the death of his father. Such people need an explanation, a justification, that may not be offered by a logical, realistic approach to life. Others are simply not intelligent enough to understand why Christianity is not a valid answer to the questions of the universe. In other words, a person of below average intelligence who was raised in a stable, normal, Christian home may not ever get around to doubting Christianity in the first place.

I am neither of the above. Although I wouldn't call my upbringing stable or normal, I can say that I was brought up in a loving environment. And although that environment was Christian, I was intelligent enough to doubt Christianity at some point.

I have not read the Bible in full—just excerpts. And the last time I read a significant portion, I was twelve. Christians will notoriously attempt to discredit non-Christians by quizzing them on the Bible. However, with the right preparation, a non-Christian can avoid this. The quickest comeback to such an attempt might be, "Have you read Newton's *Principia*[7]?" It is a cheap blow, but no cheaper than the Bible blow. Ultimately, if non-Christians are ignorant of the Bible, then Christians

---

[7]Mathematical Principles of Natural Philosophy, 1687. This famous book contains the fundamental laws of classical dynamics and gravitation.

are just as ignorant of concepts in logic and physics, generally speaking.

The next thing that must be recognized is that, as previously noted, the Bible is vague, contradictory, and fantastic. Reading only a few chapters of it is insulting to one's intelligence. However, if you are going to successfully battle Christianity, forget the Bible. Rather, target the fundamental problems in Christianity, of which the Bible is only a subset. In other words, instead of doubting the actual story of Moses parting the Red Sea, doubt the thinking process that arrives at the unbelievable, physically impossible conclusion that a person could singlehandedly part a sea.

Prophecy and *Self-Fulfilling* Prophecy

Christians have a vested interest in the success of Christianity. They have invested thousands of hours of time reading the Bible, attending church, teaching Christianity to their children, lobbying for Christian values in government, singing Christian hymns, and converting non-Christians. They have placed thousands, hundreds of thousands, even millions of dollars[8] into their pastor's collection plate over the years. They have alienated non-Christian family and friends, come to terms with their belief in miraculous, unbelievable stories—e.g.

---

[8]Consider a weekly contribution of $20. Over a period of fifty years at a weekly compounded interest rate of 5%, the total contribution is about $232,000. If a $30 weekly contribution had instead been used to defray an 8% home or car loan, the total contribution exceeds $1 million.

people walking on water—and avoided potentially enriching information that may disagree with their beliefs—e.g. cosmology.

The idea that Christianity is a human intellectual invention that has perpetuated because of its use of a scary Hell and a tempting Heaven is an infinitely heavy burden on a Christian. So, most Christians will avoid it. Unfortunately, it is already too late for most Christians.

Whether or not Christians can provide reasonable rebuttals to the concerns I have presented here—which, by the way, they rarely can—is irrelevant. The point is that they are arguing not because they have reasonable evidence in Christianity's favor, *but because they are Christian*. Most Christians cannot come up with a reasonable rebuttal because in order to arrive at one, they would have to clearly understand it. And to understand the rebuttal is to recognize the flaw in Christianity.

The same cannot be safely said about me. It should be recognized by the reader that my whole interest in writing this book is to profit from its sales. I have no self-interest in the proliferation of this information otherwise. My purpose is to provide new evidence in the acquisition of truth, because many people who are less than enamored by Christianity have often found themselves short on words or unclear in their arguments. There is not a lot of information that specifically addresses and repudiates Christianity, so it is often difficult to provide an educated response to claims like, "Jesus loves you," or "You're going to Hell, you miserable sinner. That's right, Mom, I'm talking to you." This information is valuable to many.

I hold no grudge against any Christian, and my agenda does not consist of the disestablishment of Christianity or the attack of it for attack's sake. Ultimately, I have little vested interest in the proliferation of this information.

Here's my point. I don't believe what is in this book *because* I have invested time and money into it. Rather, I have invested time and money into it *because* I believe it. And I am not too proud or stubborn to tear down everything I've ever built up if I should someday discover that my deductions were flawed.

Identity Crises

Christianity is an identity. Like any identity—Nazi, Republican, Satan worshipper, Bostonian—it becomes one's friend.

In high school, I recall a group students who always hung out together; they came from all backgrounds. One day they showed up to school in pickup trucks blasting Garth Brooks, wearing boots, cowboy hats, and jeans with plate-sized belt-buckles. And for no particular reason. It is not logical to deduce that their musical preferences all changed immediately and simultaneously. It is also not logical to conclude that they had all been hired as ranchers or cowboys. Rather, they lacked identity and a sense of self-worth, probably from poor upbringing, and attempted to find themselves in the cowboy identity.

Their identity soon became their *purpose*. They risked suspension by bringing spit cups to school. They fought anyone who called them rednecks. They worked forty hours a week to pay for their brand new oversized pickup trucks. They sacrificed their homework to play in country music bands. All for country. All for the identity.

Christianity offers the same sense of security. It bonds people. It offers them hope. It gives them purpose in life. But the price is steep. At the same time, it violently breaks bonds. It instills false hopes. Its purpose is meaningless.

Solutions

I can't claim in good faith that there is *any* viable solution to the problems with Christianity. However, I also recognize that it is infinitely easier to bitch and whine than it is to constructively criticize. I'll provide a few possibilities which, when implemented, will not correct Christianity, but could make it more useful and less dangerous to individuals and society.

First, Christianity does not rely on the stories in the Bible for its self-perpetuation. The spreading of Christianity is mainly due to the popular concepts of the love, acceptance, and forgiveness of Jesus Christ, the enticement of a pleasurable Heaven, and the fear of a painful Hell. The Bible and its stories should be completely abandoned. Since the Bible is not desperately needed for the survival of Christianity, it only serves to alienate and offend freethinkers, scientists, and philosophers.

Second, Christianity should rise above specific views and convictions—e.g. abortion and censorship. Instead, Christianity should welcome all ideas and views with equal enthusiasm. Christianity should reward clear, logical reasoning and shun gut feelings and emotion-influenced decisions.

Third, stop paying for Christianity! Turn off the TV evangelists and start taxing churches! In fact, churches should be sold and all proceeds given to the members of the church. Or, depending on the will of the members, the church should be used for the promotion of Christian values—particularly the feeding, housing, and clothing of the unfortunate. However, later in this book I will provide examples of the detriments of altruism, so I think the *best* idea is simply to sell the church. Church get-togethers should be held at members' personal residences and should consist of socializing or open discussions in which all ideas are welcomed, considered, and debated. Pastors, priests, preachers, and ministers should get a real job like the rest of us.

Fourth, Christianity should evolve strictly as a social entity and abandon its religious aspect. In other words, it should not endorse any belief at all, particularly those beliefs that are far-fetched or lack reasonable evidence. Although, if a person can provide sufficient evidence to show that the world is *not* round, for example, this evidence should not be avoided.

So what does this leave for the content of Christianity? Concededly, not much. If Christianity is to exist at all, it should consist of an environment of love, commitment, education, free and rational thought, and tolerance. It should avoid empty promises and endorsements of specific opinions.

Ironically, if these changes are implemented into its very fabric, Christianity would have a very difficult time spreading. After all, it is the judgments and empty promises and damnations that doom unsuspecting souls to Christianity. Again, the very fact that Christianity exists today is because it has taken advantage of the aspects that make it detrimental to individuals and society.

Chapter Conclusions

What are the detriments of Christianity? Christianity suffers from fundamental flaws that keep Christians in a state similar to that of the Dark Ages. Among them are evangelism, exclusivity, and ignorance. The evangelistic nature of Christianity causes only the most interesting, scary, or intuitive ideas to be spread; unfortunately, what spreads the best has *nothing* to do with its content of truth. Christians exclude those who refuse to convert, but actively welcome those who will convert, regardless of their ethics, morals, or past. Christians choose to ignore evidence that conflicts with the Bible, no matter how compelling that evidence might be. Following a "narrow path" is necessarily prejudiced.

What are the solutions to the problems with Christianity? There are many. Unfortunately, the detriments of Christianity are, in fact, the same aspects that perpetuate Christianity the best. To improve Christianity is to make it unrecognizable.

What Are the Benefits of Christianity?

This chapter will identify all of the benefits of Christianity, and it will show how Christianity improves the individual, society, and the world.

Part II

A New Perspective

Is There an Afterlife?

Is There an Afterlife?

This chapter will use the nature of one's existence to show that that existence is eternal. It also Introduces a perspective that will be helpful in answering some of time's most enduring questions.

This Philosophy

This philosophy is the result of a specific, intentional effort to discover truth. I am not quite arrogant enough to claim without reservation that the conclusions I arrive at are absolutely true. They are simply an attempt, and that attempt has resulted in a philosophical theory. That theory is outlined in this book.

Some of the evidence, arguments, and derivations may resemble those of other philosophers and mathematicians in one way or another. Philosophy students and the well-read general population may find links and similarities between this philosophy and others. However, the approach to philosophical questions taken by this book are ultimately unique, and the end product is one of a kind.

First, we will consider the question of the existence of an afterlife. What the afterlife *consists* of will not be addressed in this chapter; simply whether or not one exists is its main focus.

What is an afterlife? An afterlife, if one exists, is simply a state of consciousness that exists after one's body is dead. The afterlife does not have to--and probably does not--utilize the human body. After all, the human body is simply the physical vehicle for one's consciousness (one's existence). To conclude that there is no afterlife because one's brain dies with one's body is premature. Rather, one should ask if one is able to think or remember after his body ceases to function. That is exactly what will be asked--and then tentatively answered--by this chapter.

Fundamental Conjecture

Some will claim that simply asking the question, "Is there an afterlife?" is a flawed position. "You can't know until you die," they reason.

However, while I afford that dying will certainly provide valuable information in answering the question, it is not the *only* source of information. An analogous argument might be that one can never know how well a car is running until it breaks down. This reasoning is clearly flawed since a trained mechanic can gain valuable information by looking under the hood.

It turns out that there are other attributes to an afterlife that make its existence apparent without having to wait until death. Piece by piece, I will lead you to that conclusion, and I'll begin only with the Fundamental Conjecture and its derivations.

(I) I exist, I am conscious, and I experience.

Statement (I) is the Fundamental Conjecture. It is the one statement that is imposed on you without proof or evidence. In all regards it is unprovable, but rather is a truth discovered introspectively. Whether *I* exist is irrelevant; the truths in this book will apply to you only if *you* exist.

(II) I remember existing, being conscious, and experiencing.

Statement (II) follows directly from the Fundamental Conjecture, except that it includes the element of *recollection*. Since recollection is an observation, one need not prove such a statement. As an analogy, although I cannot prove to you that my Mom's cheesecake is the world's best, that I *observe* it to be the best is an indisputable fact.

(III) There are varying degrees of consciousness—e.g. early morning or "half-asleep" consciousness versus intense concentration consciousness.

Again, these are perceptions that aren't really debatable. You may debate whether or not *you* observe differing levels of consciousness, but I perceive myself to be sleepy sometimes and wide awake—even hyper—at other times.

(IV) If I recall an experience, then I was conscious during that experience. Equivalently, if I was unconscious during an experience—though it is not really *my* experience in such a situation—then it is reasonable to believe that I do not recall that experience.

If I do not presently recall an experience, then nothing can be said of my state of consciousness during that experience—i.e. I might or might not have been conscious.

If someday (in the future) I recall an experience, then I was conscious during that experience.

I was conscious at all the points I will ultimately (someday) remember.

Of the four truths presented so far, I imagine one might have the hardest time with statement (IV), which is also sufficiently long. Because of the formal logic required to arrive at many of the conclusions in this book, a logic review has been appended. Use it if necessary.

Note that the converse of statement (IV) is clearly false. Take, for example, the first sentence of statement

(IV). The converse is, "If I was conscious during an experience, then I recall that experience." There are sufficiently many experiences I have had that I do not recall right now. That I don't recall an experience right now says nothing of my consciousness during that experience. If today I don't get around to thinking about my high school graduation but tomorrow Mom shows me a picture and it reminds me, then it happened, and I was conscious during that experience.

Also, that I am not *able* to recall an experience right now says nothing of my consciousness at that time. Let's use the above example again, regarding my high school graduation. Yesterday, I did not think about it--hence, I did not recall it. As I've said, the fact that I didn't recall it has nothing to do with whether or not it actually occurred. Now, what if yesterday I was smoking out all day with my friends, and I was not able to remember the graduation event no matter how hard I tried? (Come to think of it, try to piece together *any* coherent memory while smoking out.) Just because I was not *able* to recall my graduation yesterday says nothing about whether the graduation actually occurred. Today I recall it, and my recollection today is evidence that it occurred.

It is important to reread the first four statements a few times and make sure that they are reasonable. I will soon be presenting a number of propositions far more debatable than these. If you have any reservations so far, don't think that they will become clearer as you read further. Get comfortable with them now and make sure you agree with them.

Experience

The Fundamental Conjecture and its derivations aside, let me pause for a moment to clarify a few concepts, particularly the concept of *experience*. These concepts will become clearer through the course of this book.

I have used the word *experience* somewhat ambiguously here; don't let it confuse you. When one is conscious, he *experiences* an event. Duh. But when one is unconscious, it doesn't really make sense to say that he experienced an event. In this case, the word *experience* refers to an event that occurred during that person's unconsciousness—a universal event, like the ticking of a clock.

Whether or not events are actually universal is irrelevant for the time being. If they aren't, then one's mind essentially *is* the world, in which case what one experiences is just what is happening. But if events are universal, then we can simply analyze a person's own virtual reality, in which her world is just what she perceives. Either way, a person cannot tell the difference between an actual world that he perceives and a virtual world that affects only him.

An experience happens in the head. To say that a sunset is an experience doesn't really make sense. Rather, a person's observation of that sunset becomes an experience. An experience is not just what appears to physically happen. An experience is what one perceives from any number of stimuli, some physical, some mental. A real, naked woman is not necessarily superior to a juicy fantasy. Both cause the observer to experience. Just because Marylou fantasizes about Tom Cruise while having sex with her boyfriend, Harold, does not imply that her fantasy "really" occurred. However, the experience that she will ultimately recall—her fantasy of Tommy boy—*did* occur.

Virtual Reality Still-Frame Perspective

The philosophy presented in this book derives its power from the Virtual Reality Still-Frame perspective. The origin of the "virtual reality" part of that view should be relatively clear now: we are observing consciousness from a person's eyes, ears, nose, tongue, and fingers. Whether or not a tree actually exists is irrelevant in this perspective; all that matters is that one sees it and is affected by it.

But don't we all see the same tree? Of course not. Consider, for example, its color. It's green—okay, we agree on that. But when you see green, what do you see? The tree might appear to you what I would perceive as red. But we don't disagree since the color you perceive as red you call green. Today's fashions might, from your perspective, appear what I would call bright, obnoxious, clashing colors But you wouldn't use those words to describe them since bright, obnoxious, and clashing refer to the easy, laid-back, pales that I observe. In other words, maybe what we perceive as fashion doesn't refer to the quality of the wardrobes at all, but rather to their evolutionary ability to replicate, the concept "good fashion" *resulting* from what wins out in competition. As far as I know, technology has no method for observing what color I see when I look at green.

The color green might affect you differently than it does me. So although we both agree that green light corresponds to a very specific light wavelength, you have no idea what I *see* when I see green.

What was the best sex of your life? Think back. Give a name. A place. A position. Don't worry, I won't tell. Just answer me this: are you sure it actually happened? "I've got the underwear to prove it." How do you know the underwear exists? "I felt the orgasm and it was fantastic." How do you know that a mad scientist wasn't simply probing into your brain during a routine dental check-up and accidentally touched the orgasm-creating neurons? "Well, I remember the experience." *How do you know that the memory wasn't simply implanted in your head?*

Total Recall is a pretty good brainteaser on this subject, if you can really follow what's going on. The idea is that the memory of a great vacation is implanted into a person's mind at a much lower cost than an actual comparable vacation. Even though the person remembers visiting such virtual reality "travel agents," he cannot tell that his vacation was not real. Thus the "still-frame" aspect of my philosophy is revealed: one cannot tell whether his memories represent actual experiences or if he became conscious at the present and was simultaneously instilled with memories of experiences.

The still-frame refers to the fact that it is always now; it is never the past and never the future. Experiences don't occur in the past or the future; they occur in the present. The Virtual Reality Still-Frame consciousness is an observational existence that is always just beginning and never getting older but increasing in its possession of memories. The Virtual Reality Still-Frame is a useful perspective in learning what is absolutely true and what is just apparently true.

From this perspective, I don't know that the sky exists. I only know that I observe the sky to exist. I also don't know that I sang in the shower this morning. I only know that I observe a memory of singing in the shower this morning. From a virtual reality perspective, what I observe may or may not really be true; it doesn't really matter. What matters is that I observe. I know that I observe. From the still-frame perspective, what I remember may or may not have actually happened; again, it doesn't really matter. What matters is that I remember. I know I remember.

The Virtual-Reality Still-Frame perspective is conservative, to say the least. Many philosophers may believe that this is a step in the wrong direction, since it basically repudiates all information that is gathered empirically. Although it is conservative, its conclusions are more certain since its skeptical viewpoint accepts less on faith.

There is information, I believe, that can be gleaned from this perspective. Among that information is the existence of an afterlife, Heaven, Hell, and the future of pleasure and pain.

Stream of Consciousness

From the virtual reality standpoint, I am never unconscious, since it requires a conscious thought to observe that I am unconscious, a clear paradox. I observe time to be continuous, and the less conscious I am—

recognizing that there are various levels of consciousness—the slower time appears to me in relation to "absolute" points of reference (if, indeed, such points of reference exist). The simplest example of this is deep sleep. Ever lie down to bed after a rough day and (what appears to be) only a few minutes later your morning alarm clock sounds? Even though many hours appeared to pass in someone else's frame of reference—like the night clerk at a Circle K—only a minute or two appeared to pass in yours. In that regard, your consciousness was continuous, with the possible exception of a point discontinuity.

Similarly, sleeping in on a bright, warm Saturday will often result in numerous dreams, but the total time observed to pass in these dreams is far less than the actual time passed, because dreaming is a very low level of consciousness. You know how it is. You crack your neck and part your sticky eyelids to glance at the LED clock: "Oh, just nine," you think. "I've got time." You close your eyes and dream a one- or two-minute dream, and when you open your eyes its eleven.

(V) I am constantly conscious.

A common rebuttal to this claim will come from scientists who claim that I am not conscious during sleep. Therefore, I am not constantly conscious. I agree, with a certain reservation. As I've mentioned, this conclusion results from the Virtual-Reality Still-Frame perspective. From my point of view, it appears as if I fall asleep and then immediately wake up. There is no way for me to know *for sure* that the scientist who was watching me sleep didn't in fact trick me into believing that I was unconscious. It is not very plausible, but the point is that I can't know for sure. From my observation, I am constantly conscious because I am never consciously observing my own state of unconsciousness. I certainly believe that others can observe me to sleep, just as I can observe others to sleep. But from my observation, I am always conscious.

This concept is not particularly complex. Try not to dote on it too long, unless you really don't understand it. I provide no proof for the "stream of consciousness" because it is virtually by the definition of the Virtual-Reality Still-Frame perspective that one's consciousness is continuous.

Memory and Consciousness

At your twenty-first birthday, your friends—and I use the word *friends* very relatively here—decide to get you tanked. Unfortunately, the party didn't really start until after that thirteenth shot of Bacardi 151 hit you. Too bad. Consider three possibilities.

Number one. You remember the entire night. My only response: damn, can you hold your booze.

Number two. You don't remember a thing. Your buddies ask, "Don't you remember hooking up with that sorority girl?" You close your eyes, clench your fists, and try with all your might to remember. After a few hours, everything has come back to you. Perhaps a little fuzzy, but you've got most of the night mapped out.

At the very least, you *were* conscious during your birthday, if only partially, as evidenced by the fact that you eventually recalled it. Even if it was dream-like, you did have some concept of time during the party.

Number three. You try and try to recall your birthday but you can't. You try again the next day and can't. You try again next week and can't. Ultimately, you are never (ever) capable of recalling the events of that night. Here's the question: how much time did you measure elapse on your birthday from the moment that last shot hit you until the time you awoke the next morning? From your virtual reality standpoint, none. It is as if your mind (your consciousness) skipped over the event.

Whether the event actually occurred, and any time passed at all, is also debatable, and for all practical purposes unknowable. After all, the only information one ever receives is through observation. If you didn't observe the party first-hand, then (according to the Virtual-Reality Still-Frame perspective), there is no way to know for absolute sure that the party even happened. It is at least conceivable that your friends played a horrible trick on you... they drugged you with nitrous oxide, threw some fake vomit on the floor, reset the clock, dumped a beer on your shirt, pounded you on the head a few times to induce a headache, et cetera. Maybe there wasn't a party after all.

If you are never (ever) able to recall the party, then from your perspective, the party never even occurred.

"But, Andrew, this is absurd. The party did happen, because you told me about it. There were observers there, and they all told me about how I got drunk, had sex with a hot girl, then fell asleep." Unfortunately, all of your information came from observers *other than yourself*. Let me ask this. Did dinosaurs roam the earth millions of years ago? Yes? How do you know? Were you an observer? It is just a story that you accept because the physical evidence (that others have discovered and presented) is reasonably convincing. But you have no first-hand memory of the dinosaurs. You will never have first-hand memory of the dinosaurs. It is as if your consciousness *skipped over* the Jurassic period to the time when you were born. Just because you didn't observe it doesn't mean that it didn't happen; it just means that from your Virtual-Reality Still-Frame perspective, it didn't happen.

So, getting back to the party example, if you are never, ever, ever able to remember what happened on the night of your party, it is as if the party never happened, from your perspective. The only thing you will ultimately observe (in relation to your party) is the story your friends told you. You will remember your friends' story, but you will not remember the party. Your consciousness didn't skip over your friends' story, but it appears to have skipped over your party.

In a moment, I'm going to present another example, one which is fundamental to this philosophical theory. But understanding the above example is necessary to understand the next example. Make sure you agree with it. Is it reasonable?

Again, I am not claiming that the party didn't happen. But I am claiming that, because you will never remember the party, you will never know *for sure* that the party happened--i.e. that your friends weren't playing a prank on you.

It is as if your consciousness just skipped over the party.

The Omnipotent Sadist

Let's make a deal.

I am a sadist. I would get great sexual satisfaction by kicking your ass. But I am also a considerate capitalist, so I will offer you money for this satisfaction. The deal goes like this.

I will subject you to immense physical pain for ten minutes. Afterwards, you will be operated on by the world's best plastic surgeon, who will restore your body to exactly how it was before the torture. Then, your brain will be probed by the world's best brain neurologist, who will completely erase from your mind the memory of the torture. All you will remember is making a deal with me and then receiving payment.

What is your price? A mil? A grand? What about $50?

What if the torture were to last not ten minutes, but ten seconds? Now what is your price? What about one second, or a fraction of a second?

When one mulls over this example for a while, it becomes apparent that it *doesn't really matter* how long the torture lasts. Let's say that the deal also included a promise to restore your life to exactly how it was before the torture. The torture could last for a year, but it wouldn't make any difference to the observer. All the observer would perceive is making a deal with the Omnipotent Sadist and then immediately having a stash of bills in his hand. It would appear to be free money.

Some will object. "You are still subjecting me to pain, even if I immediately forget about, so that pain has a price--an *enormous* price."

What difference does it make to one now how much pain she has felt in the past? If yesterday she spent all day throwing up, what difference does that pain make to her today? Well, she remembers it. And she will remember not to drink so much vodka in the future. In other words, the memory serves a purpose, and it is meaningful, but she is not experiencing any pain today as a result of the pain she felt yesterday. So what difference does it make to her today if yesterday she entered into the above contract with me? What difference would it make to her today if yesterday she was subjected to intense torture? The only difference it would make is that today she is $5 richer (or whatever the agreed-upon price was).

I recognize that most people are more productive than $5 a day, so let me again remind you of the stipulation that I would have to restore her life to exactly how it was before the torture. In that regard, she has lost no time, and she is $5 richer. More information regarding pleasure and pain will be presented in later chapters.

Another objection might be that, "Andrew, you didn't torture me *yesterday*. The deal you are offering is to torture me right now. And right now I can experience pain." Agreed. But keep in mind that you will completely forget about the pain. Let's say the torture was to begin at 12:00 and end at 12:10, and by 12:15 all will be forgotten and restored. Well, I think you would agree that 12:15 will come. It's not like time would freeze eternally during the torture. By someone else's watch, 12:15 will come. And at 12:15 you will have permanently forgotten about the torture. Your consciousness will have appeared to have completely skipped over the event. It will appear to you, from your Virtual-Reality Still-Frame perspective, that the event never happened.

If one is about to enter a "time period" which he will ultimately forget forever, he would observe no time passing during that period, his mind would skip over it, and he would find himself conscious in the next point which does not have such a characteristic. In other words, if, starting tomorrow, you would ultimately forget everything that happened today, *you would already be there*.

Tonight, when you are deep asleep (and not dreaming), prove me wrong. Say, "Hey, Andrew, you're wrong. I'm completely unconscious right now, I'll never remember saying this, and the next time I'll be conscious is at 6:45 when my alarm clock sounds. Since I'm not there yet, you better rethink your book a little."

Certainly such a rebuttal isn't reasonable, since it would require consciousness both to perform such a task, as well as to remember it in order to tell me about it.

Recalling Experiences

Consider another example: birth. Before some point—say, my birth—I was not conscious. Since I was unconscious, I will never recall the events that occurred before my birth. Clearly, I observe no time elapsed between the beginning of time[1] and my birth. So, even though years and years and years and years progressed, as measured by other observers (like the dinosaurs) my consciousness skipped over these years and my next (and first) observation was from some point around 1980, when I was three years old.

Let's try one more simply example just to ice the cake. Assume that there is a place called Fantasy Land, an actual business where all your sexual dreams come true. There is no charge, but there is one specific stipulation: each sex act (and orgasm) only lasts a second[2], and the moment it is over you will permanently forget about it. Would you go? Would it be worth your time to go to Fantasy Land? Just think about it for a few. When you leave the establishment, you will take nothing with you, including memories. Would it have any meaning at all?

My answer, and hopefully yours, is no. If you spent twenty years there, then it would appear as if your consciousness skipped over those years, and it would already be twenty years later. You would look in the mirror and notice that you look twenty years older, but you wouldn't have twenty years worth of memories. The

---

[1]Possibly the Big Bang

[2]Ladies, does this sound familiar?

last thing you would remember would be what happened twenty years before. It would appear as if your consciousness was continuous, and skipped right over the time that you ultimately (and permanently) forgot.

The above examples, as well as years of introspection, have led me to the following conclusion, statement (VI).

(VI) If I ultimately (and permanently) forget an event, then my consciousness appears to have skipped over that event. Equivalently, if my consciousness does not appear to have skipped over an event, then I will remember that event.

The first part of statement (VI) is just what we have established with the previous examples. The second part is just its contrapositive, which is why it is preceded with the word *equivalently*. What does it mean "if my consciousness does not appear to have skipped over an event?" It just means that I am conscious. Certainly, if one is conscious during an event, then it does not appear to that person that his consciousness skipped over that event. So, the second part of statement (VI) claims that any time a person is conscious of an event, she will remember that event, at least once.

From this, we can logically show that *all* conscious experiences must be recalled, at least once.

(i) If I ultimately forget an event, then I ultimately observe no time elapsed during that event, and I ultimately observe my consciousness to have skipped over that event.

(ii) While "experiencing" such an event, my next observation will be from the *next* point that I am conscious.
(iii) My consciousness is continuous.
(iv) So, I do not experience such events.
(v) Finally, the events that I experience will all be recalled.

(VII) I will recall all of my experiences.

If you have followed all of my arguments and derivations so far, and you find the propositions and examples reasonable, then the remaining conclusions in this book will fall easily into place. Probably the most important conclusion so far, from which the existence of an afterlife and the nonexistence of Heaven and Hell can be derived, is this: if I was conscious during an event, then I will remember that event. Equivalently, if I will not remember an event (ever), then I was unconscious (or *not* conscious) during that event.

The second statement (*equivalently*...) is not so easy to buy. Even though it is logically equivalent to a statement that has been well established so far, it states that if there is an event that you will ultimately forget, then you couldn't have consciously observed it in the first place. More will be discussed later on the subject of cause-and-effect, but for now it suffices to say that the two statements are equivalent. So if you agree that, "If I was conscious during an event, then I will remember that event," then you should also agree that, "If I will not remember an event, then I was unconscious during that event."

Afterlife and Recollection

Let's say that someday you acquire a horrible case of permanent amnesia--so bad, in fact, that you never again remember anything that happened prior to that amnesia. Call it complete permanent amnesia.

Using the previous conclusions in this chapter and what we have assumed of the imaginary disease complete permanent amnesia, I will attempt to logically show that an afterlife exists.

(i) If I get complete permanent amnesia at some point T in the future, then I would observe the time to be at or later than T right now, since I am presently a conscious observer[3].
(ii) I do not observe time to be at or later than T right now.
(iii) So, I will not get complete permanent amnesia at T.
(iii) I will die—physically, at the very least.
(iv) So, my death will not result in complete permanent amnesia.
(v) I will recall memories after my death.
(vi) I must be conscious to recall.
(vii) I will be conscious after death.
(viii) So, my consciousness will not end after death; there is an afterlife.

---

[3]This is because my consciousness skips over all events that I ultimately and permanently forget. So, if at time T, I forgot everything that ever happened until T, then the next point I would consciously observe would be T.

(VIII) There is an afterlife.

Try to imagine experiencing complete permanent amnesia. It would be the same in all regards to being born—after all, birth is simply a case of complete permanent amnesia from the Virtual-Reality Still-Frame perspective. You wouldn't be able to speak, and you wouldn't know what things were. As a consciousness receiving only (what appeared to be) random signals, you would not associate any information to the light that pierced your eyes or the sounds that vibrated your eardrums. You would not know what a human body was or even that you possessed (and potentially controlled) one. You would be a baby. Your first thoughts would be just that: your first. You were never before conscious. If you existed prior to being born, then you were *unconscious*.

(i) By (IV), if I will remember an event, then I was conscious at that event. Equivalently, if I was unconscious during an event, then I will never remember that event.
(ii) By (VI), if I will ultimately forever forget an event, then I was unconscious during that event. Equivalently, if I am conscious during an event, I will remember that event.
(iii) By (i) and (ii), we arrive at (IX)[4].

---

[4]Again, this is a logical conclusion. If this bothers you, take a look at Appendix A: Logic Refresher.

(IX) I am conscious during an event if and only if I will recall the event. I am unconscious during an event if and only if I will never recall the event.

I've had great reservations about using the words *conscious* and *unconscious* since their usage is so widely distributed among meanings. We return to the story about your twenty-first birthday. The very fact that you will never remember it *requires* that you were unconscious. But don't confuse this with a cause-and-effect relationship. A tree is green when you look at it. But that does not imply that the tree is green *because* you looked at it, or that the tree turned green *when* you looked at it. But that you observe it to be green requires that it is green—that is, of course, assuming that the tree exists at all!

The fact that you ultimately forget an event does not *cause* it to be unconscious. After all, at the time of the event, you were either conscious or unconscious, regardless of whether or not you ultimately remember it in the future. But if you were unconscious, you will not ever recall it, and if you were conscious, you must (someday) recall it. Whether or not you ultimately recall the event is simply an *indicator* of whether you were conscious or not; it is not what *determines* whether you were conscious or not.

Chapter Conclusions

Is my consciousness continuous? Other observers will say no, but then again, I am only observing them say no. From the Virtual-Reality Still-Frame perspective, it appears as if my consciousness is continuous because I cannot consciously observe being in a state of unconsciousness.

Which memories will I ultimately recall? All of them. Every conscious experience must be recalled at least once.

Is there an afterlife? Here, the word *afterlife* refers to an ability to have experiences after one's physical body and brain have permanently ceased functioning. The evidence in this chapter reasonably shows that there *is* an afterlife.

Exercises

Virtual Reality

Problem #1: You're a raging alcoholic. One night, in a barren meadow, you get all tanked up. You tear off your clothes and do many unbelievable, immoral things that common decency prevents me from describing. You stumble back to your clothes, throw them on, and pass out. In the morning, you don't remember anything—in fact, you will ultimately *never* remember the events of that night—and there were no witnesses. Did the event happen?

Afterlife

Problem #2: Using only statement (VII)[1]—and common sense—prove the existence of an afterlife.

[1] I will recall all of my experiences.

Solutions

Answer #1: The assumption is that you will never know what happened that night, and it ultimately did not affect you in any way. From the virtual reality standpoint, it did not happen. Although this seems inconsistent with the fact that I stated in Problem #1 that it *did* occur, keep in mind that the situation is hypothetical and if it were true, I wouldn't know about it.

Answer #2:
(i) I will recall all of my experiences.
(ii) Recalling is an experience.
(iii) So, I will recall recalling an experience, and recall recalling the recollection of an experience… and on.
(iv) So, I will recall an experience infinitely.
(v) I cannot recall an experience infinitely within one lifetime.
(vi) There is an afterlife.

Is Time Travel Possible?

Is Time Travel Possible?

This chapter will apply the Virtual-Reality Still-Frame perspective and the conclusions derived in the last chapter to numerous contemporary questions, including fate versus free will and the possibility of time travel.

Materialism vs. Dualism

A common debate on the subject of consciousness —and one that has thrust itself in the forefront of science—is whether one's existence ("soul") is separate from the physical brain. There is little debate that they are intimately related. The brain sends messages to one's consciousness, which makes decisions and sends commands back to the brain. There isn't *always* this relationship. The brain can "act" on its own, such as in response to touching a hot iron. Also, one may not consciously notice many of the millions of signals received from the body at any given time. After all, when you are sitting, your backside neurons are constantly sending touch information to your brain, but how often do you think about the feeling of your tush against your chair?

Very simplistically, one class is called the Materialists—those who believe that the brain is the *source* of one's consciousness, and the other is the Dualists—those who see consciousness as "something more."

This philosophy endorses dualism. I believe I have shown that my physical death will not result in the death of my consciousness, or of my ability to recall or think. The "stuff" that is capable of recalling, thinking, and introspection is exactly my soul, my consciousness, and my identity. Because it will not perish upon physical death, my brain is *not* the source of my consciousness, and so my consciousness is something more. I do not claim to understand this state of being, which is clearly not physical, and I offer no explanation. But I have not given up on the search for an answer. My adoption of the philosophy of dualism is not, as Daniel Dennett claims in *Consciousness Explained*, "just accepting defeat without admitting it."

Since I only know that *my* consciousness is eternal, and since my physical body is not yet dead, it is at least conceivable that I am "immortal." This would satisfy both the arguments in this book as well as of the Materialists: my brain is the source of my consciousness, but my brain will never die. However, I only mention this to exhaust all possibilities; I admit that it is patently absurd.

It may also be comforting for Materialists to believe that my proof for the existence of an afterlife was motivated by an evolutionary urge to believe that life isn't a complete waste. Because let's face it. If the Humanist and Materialist are correct, and all we are is dust in the wind, then all we have accomplished, all we will do, all we will experience, and all we will love, will all be dirt someday. Not an exciting thought, to say the least. So maybe this book is entirely a self-gratifying, self-convincing treatise that I am not "wasting my time," that my life matters.

I will thwart that possibility immediately.

Consciousness is either eternal, or it is not. Certainly any logical reader would agree on these two mutually exclusive possibilities. But *neither* possibility is desirable. If you think that living forever is a privilege, then you don't have a clear concept of eternity. Eternity is not an extra hour in the day. It is not one more weekend at the beach. It is not an additional week to spend with a loved one. It is not one more month to finish that garage project. It is not just one more year to spend with the grandkids. It is not another lifetime to start anew. It is not ten lifetimes, or a hundred, or a million. When you are so god-damned tired of waking up in the morning, you can sleep and sleep and sleep until you can't sleep anymore... and then you'll wake up again. I don't want to live forever but I don't have any choice. I can't toss my cards on the table and put out my cigar. I can't file Chapter 7. I'm in it for good and no matter how many Materialists try to save me from the grips of Eternity, they failed from the moment of my conception.

Complete Permanent Amnesia

There are applications of this philosophical theory. One of them, believe it or not, deals with the law. Let's reconsider the imaginary disease mentioned before, complete permanent amnesia.

Many people fear "dying before they die." Most people who occasionally visit nursing homes are awed by how lifeless they are: not physically, but mentally. Where did those eighty years' worth of memories go? If a person can't recall any past experiences, then those experiences—much like the tree falling in a deserted wood—are meaningless. So observers are frightened into cherishing their memories before senility, amnesia, insanity, or Alzheimer's disease set in. Luckily, there is a cure: time. As shown in *Is There an Afterlife?*, no memories are ever lost, so long as the holder of those memories was conscious when they were made. A soul may not regain its sanity or memories until after death, since the physical body clearly has an effect on one's mental state, but they will be regained eventually.

After a bad automobile accident, many amnesia patients claim they do not remember anything one minute, ten minutes, an hour, even a day before the actual accident. When this occurs, the victim is relieved of extensive court testimony in a civil or criminal lawsuit, and witnesses to the accident must be utilized to discover the truth. There are only two mutually exclusive possibilities.

(1) The victim will at some time in the future recall the time in question.
(2) The victim will never remember the time in question.

If statement (1) is correct, then the victim's insurance company should simply wait until the victim can remember what happened. Civil lawsuits can be filed in most American states up to twenty years after the liability occurred. It is highly unlikely that a person not remember a significant memory within twenty years after the memory was made.

However, if statement (2) is correct, then the person could not have been conscious at the time in question. He was either sloppy drunk or asleep. Both cases would make the patient liable.

If neither of these is the case, then the person is simply lying. He believes that the accident was his fault and knows that claiming amnesia would give him a better shot at winning a lawsuit, since he would not have to testify against himself.

So, if a person claims amnesia in an accident lawsuit, and does not "remember" (or admit) the truth within a reasonable amount of time, then that person was most likely the cause of the accident, *whether or not* he is telling the truth about his amnesia.

Fate vs. Free Will

Can anything about the future be known? There are really only two mutually exclusive possibilities: either the future is set in stone, or it is not. I know that I will always exist, ad infinitum—or, more appropriately, *ad eternitum*. So there are at least some things that can be known about the future. But such evidence does not wholly prove that the future is set in stone. And even if it is set in stone, this evidence does not show that the future can be wholly known. After all, if, for example, you knew that you were going to get wasted tonight and kill your best friend in a gruesome car accident, you probably would reconsider your rendezvous with Captain Morgan tonight. Thus, the accident wouldn't happen and, in retrospect, you really *didn't* know what was going to happen tonight.

So maybe it is possible to know only those things that you cannot change or affect. I certainly can't decide one day to stop existing, so the fact that I know about my afterlife does not cause any problems.

Most scientists subscribe to basic cause-and-event logic, where things happen because of preceding events. If so, then every event is completely predictable and unavoidable. In that regard, everything that has happened or ever will happen is set in stone: time is fated in god's favorite storybook. But even the most meticulous scientist has a hard time arguing against our concept of free will. "Conscious minds are somehow different," he rationalizes. “They don't have to respond to previous events. They can make conscious choices."

I just shouted "You need to pay your income taxes!" No kidding; I really did. No one could have predicted it. Even my girlfriend, or my mother. I hate the IRS; I am ethically opposed to our federal government. So I did what I did in a desperate attempt to be unpredictable. But some might still argue that I failed at defying fate. They might say, "Andrew, you're writing a book on philosophy. You're talking about predictability and cause-and-event relationships. Anyone could have predicted that you would try to do something unpredictable. One thing led to another, so the only possible thing you could have done at that moment was shout, *You need to pay your income taxes!*"

So whether or not time is ultimately fated, or perhaps just partially fated, is not within the scope of this book. But, in response to my earlier question, *can anything about the future be known?* A wholehearted yes. Many things, in fact. On that note, I'll apply this philosophy to time travel.

Time Travel

Time travel backward, if possible, would have some nightmarish and paradoxical implications. Time travel forward is okay—we don't run into any problems. But time travel backward would get particularly interesting when (and the word *when* is used here very relatively) a person decides to kill his former self. What would happen then? If the person is dead, then he can't possibly go back in time to kill his former self. But if he lives, then he'll go back in time to kill his former self, which would keep him from going back in time to kill his former self... You get the idea. And the paradox doesn't even have to be so direct.

What if, in the year 2001, Herbert travels back in time to the year 1800 and ends up in a deserted meadow? Well, as he walks through the meadow, all the butterflies flutter away to an adjacent meadow, which happens to be the future location of Tampa, Florida. Naturally, the butterflies procreate as swiftly as an Alachua County welfare mother, and two hundred years later there are a billion more butterflies in Tampa than if Herbie had never traveled back in time. One day in the year 2000, Herb is crossing a street when a swarm of butterflies attracts his attention. So, he stops, looks, and gets run over by a Hyundai, speeding well in excess of 30 miles per hour (quite a feat for a Hyundai). Since he didn't live to travel back in time, the same paradox occurs. Chaos theorists have coincidentally named this the *butterfly effect*; not the actual story, but the general idea. They say that the mere beating of a butterfly's wings can have monstrous effects on the future.

However, to my knowledge, no one has successfully proven that time travel backward is impossible. Here's my contribution to the debate.

We can define at least two types of time travel: one that includes me (*inclusive*) and one that doesn't (*exclusive*). The first deals with altering my own time, while the second deals with altering everyone else's time and observing the effects. Therefore, four possible travel schemes exist: forward exclusively and inclusively, and backward exclusively and inclusively. We'll consider each of them.

Traveling forward exclusively. Here, the observer measures less time passed than those he is observing do. The observer does not age, but everyone else does. On a purely mental level, people experience this sort of time travel every day: sleep. If you sleep on a Greyhound bus through a 60-mile journey, you may not perceive the entire six-hour travel time, whereas the bus driver will—in most cases, anyway. If you don't want to experience something, sleep through it. When you wake up, it may feel as if only a few minutes have passed, but really it may be many hours later. In this example, one's body still ages. But can one's body travel forward exclusively, too? Yes.

Biologically, suspended animation is going to be the craze of the next millennium. Theoretically, suspended animation induces a deep sleep in a person's body, which slows both the body's and mind's aging. A person could be revived from such a state after fifty years and find himself younger—in body and mind—than her own grandchildren. Because of the risks involved with such a scientifically undeveloped process, most American states do not allow the cryogenic preservation of a living person, even with that person's consent—in much the same way that suicide is illegal in most states. However, there are profit corporations that make a business of cryogenically preserving the "freshly" dead. Their rationale? A person who is legally dead by today's medical standards may be revivable with the medicine of tomorrow. Simply keep the mind and body from deteriorating further until a cure or medical procedure can be perfected which restores that person's life. I don't know if it will work—no one legally dead has yet been revived by such logic—but such cryonicists lend credence to the thought of exclusive forward time travel through suspended animation.

Einstein in his Special Theory of Relativity first proposed the interrelationship between space and time. Time is not absolute, a fact that can be, and has been, experimentally verified. If I were to move away from you at near the speed of light, turn around, and come back, I would measure significantly less time elapsed than you would. It all depends on how fast I moved with respect to you, and “how long” (an obviously relative phrase) I was gone. It is conceivable that after a one-year trip by my watch, I could return to an Earth that had aged a billion years. (How big would our brains be by then?) Or maybe the Earth and sun wouldn't even exist anymore. Interestingly enough, the science, technology, and materials exist today that could build such a “time machine.” Granted, such a project would require unsurpassed manpower and an incredible amount of raw materials, but it could be done. After all, who'd have thought that humans could walk on the moon with just ten years' dedication?

So, traveling forward exclusively is possible using at least two different technologies. Either way, the observer measures less time progressed than those he is observing. Because he measures less time, he can recall fewer experiences (relativistic time travel) or no experiences (biological time travel) within the time in question.

Traveling forward inclusively. Let's think really hard about this one. A person travels forward through time and has no disagreements with those he observes concerning how much time has elapsed. Is there smoke coming out of your ears? Don't strain your brain. This situation is definitely possible; it happens all the time. It's called *life*. Conscious souls are constantly traveling forward inclusively through time.

Traveling backward exclusively. This isn't the same as looking back in time, which is no problem. The light that we receive from a star which is a hundred million light-years away is exactly a hundred million years old. So when we look out into the universe, we are looking back in time. But can you actually experience, or become a part of, time that has already occurred?

This is the situation I described using the butterfly analogy. Scientists have not completely ruled out this possibility yet. Some physicists even claim that by dilating a wormhole and accelerating through it to near the speed of light, time outside of the wormhole would appear to reverse. In one form, Einstein's Special Theory seems to support this concept[1]. But, then again, the same theory precludes the possibility of a physical object reaching or exceeding the speed of light.

The only way that exclusive backward time travel could be possible, while avoiding space-time paradoxes, is if what occurred in the observed past had no bearing on the observer's future. This would endorse the concept of parallel universes. So Herbert could go back in time and kill his former self, but that former self isn't really him! It's just one of infinitely many other Herberts that existed simultaneously in one of infinitely many parallel universes. Or something like that.

---

[1]Time slows down as one approaches the speed of light. Time stops at the speed of light. Conclusion? Time reverses as one exceeds the speed of light.

Traveling backward inclusively. Say I build a time machine that is designed to reverse the time of everyone inside, including me. One could easily deduce that time would stand still right at the moment that I turned it on. Why? Because the cycle would repeat itself ad infinitum. I would never know that I was caught up in such a time cycle. Every time I turned on the time machine, I would perceive that I was turning it on for the first time, so there would be no reason for me not to turn it on every time I reached that point in time. Since my consciousness could not progress beyond that single point in time, I would be incapable of being conscious at some point in the future beyond that "infinite" point. Clearly, that violates statements (VII) and (IX).

(X) I will never travel backward in time inclusively.

Chapter Conclusions

Are the Dualists correct? Yes. The permanence of my consciousness requires that no physical death can halt or kill it. Although it appears that there is some relationship between the soul and the brain—they affect each other—they do not depend on each other and are therefore separate entities.

Is permanent amnesia or memory loss possible? No. Here, we assume that only a conscious person can make a memory, which implies that the memory must be recalled at least once after the memory lapse. At any given time, a conscious soul must be able to recall all of his memories at least once more. So permanent amnesia or memory loss is not possible.

Is it possible to build a time machine? To travel forward? Yes. To travel backward? Probably not. But it can be safely said that it is not possible to reverse one's *own* time.

Exercises

Materialism

Problem #1: Materialists will claim that consciousness depends on the physical existence of the brain. They may claim that although the Fundamental Conjecture is valid now, it will not be valid when one dies. Therefore, the proof regarding the existence of an afterlife is invalid. Rebut this argument.

Free Will

Problem #2: Is your will free?

(a) If so, are there some external causes which affect you *against your will*?
(b) If not, then what force determines your fate? Chance, god, or cause-and-effect? Is your fate predictable?

Solutions

Answer #1: The conclusions in the chapter are derived from the truth of the Fundamental Conjecture *right now*. The requirement that I must recall all of my experiences is independent of *everything*, except that I was conscious when I experienced. My consciousness doesn't seem to care that my brain is going to die at some point. If my consciousness were to end with it, this would preclude the possibility of my being conscious *ever*. Even if I have been conscious for only one second, my consciousness is eternal.

Answer #2: (varies)

Does God Exist?

In this chapter, we will apply the Virtual Reality/Still Frame perspective to analyze some philosophical questions.

Oh, God!

Descartes would have us believe that god exists because the cause of Descartes' existence and ideas must be at least as real as his existence and ideas, themselves. For example, he could not have a concept of infinity unless some infinite cause inspired that idea. That infinite cause must be god. Unfortunately, such a claim requires a cause-and-effect relationship between all things existing in the universe. If such a relationship always existed, then the following proof would be valid.

(i) The world (universe) is an effect.
(ii) Something caused it.
(iii) God caused it.
(iv) I did not cause it[1].
(v) I am not god.
(vi) God exists, and is not me.

But such a relationship gets a little confusing when one questions the cause of god.

(vii) God is an effect.
(viii) Something caused it.
(ix) God's mother caused it.
(x) So, god's mother is god.
(xi) See (vii).

Using a cause-and-effect relationship argument, it then seems difficult to show the existence of god. Maybe we should first consider the larger picture—the existence of an external world—of which the concept of god would surely be a subset.

External World

If there is no external world, then there can be no external god, so god can't exist. Therefore, we must first determine whether or not there is an external world.

I would claim that there is an external world,

---

[1]See Problem #1 in the Exercises following this chapter.

simply because it would be impossible for me to learn anything if only I existed. I think it is fair to deduce that only an external world could be the source of my knowledge. Following is a logical argument that attempts to show this.

(i) I have learned things.
(ii) I can learn things through self-inquiry or methods other than self-inquiry.
(iii) If I learn through some method other than self-inquiry, then there exists an external world.
(iv) If I know something, I cannot inquire into it.
(v) If I do not know something, I cannot inquire into it.
(vi) So, I cannot inquire into things[2].
(vii) I learn through some method other than self-inquiry.
(viii) So, there is an external world.

Are you agreeable with the postulates? If so, it follows from the above argument and the conclusions from *Is There an Afterlife?* that an external world will always exist (or, at least, that there will be an external world in the future, too).

(ix) Learning is an experience. I will recall (or relive) that experience again, say at time T.
(x) I can only relive that experience by learning, and I can only learn from an external world.
(x) So, there will be an external world at time T.
(xi) Time T was chosen arbitrarily, so there will always

---

[2]The essentials of Meno's Paradox are represented by statements (iv) through (vi).

be an external world in the future.

(XXI) There is a world external to me.

Socrates would object to statement (i) above. He believed that when a person perceived the sensation of learning, he was simply remembering something that he knew previously. But this can't be the case.

(i) I will relive the experience of learning over and over again as time progresses.
(ii) So, I will know infinitely many things--i.e. everything--by the end of eternity.
(iii) Assume: the perception of learning something is caused by remembering it.
(iv) So, I know everything now.
(v) My mind is infinite.
(vi) My mind is not infinite[3]. Contradiction with (v), so statement (iii) is false.

And since I will never reach the end of eternity, my mind will never be infinite, which is in harmony with the fact that I will continuously learn new things.

Zombies

I'm not the only thing in existence. So, there *is* the possibility that god and other people exist. But what does it mean for another person to exist? Her body? Her mind? Her soul? Well, something about her exists

---

[3]See Problem #3 in the Exercises following this chapter.

because I can learn something from her in the form of knowledge and experiences. But this form of existence is no different than the way a dog, a spider, or a grain of sand exist. Is there something more real about a person's existence than a dog's? If there is, then it must be found in that person's consciousness. The fact that consciousness clearly separates a physical being from its introspective *existence* is commonly explained using the word *zombie*.

A zombie is a person that talks, walks, works, plays, and in every regard appears to exist, but lacks identity and the ability of introspection. A well-built and well-programmed robot, for example, might fool people into believing that it is human, but it clearly is not. The robot is a zombie because it cannot think for itself, it is not conscious, and it ultimately does not exist (except as a robot).

Reciprocally, my body exists only in that I can learn things—experience new sensations—from and about it. But it does not have its own consciousness. Only I do. I know I exist, because I am conscious—the Fundamental Conjecture re-visited.

So, is it possible to tell the difference between a conscious individual and a zombie? First, consider a person who exists.

(i) Assume: Birtha exists.
(ii) Birtha is conscious.
(iii) Birtha's consciousness is defined by the sensations she receives[4].

---

[4]This will be shown in a later chapter.

(iv) I cannot experience exactly the same sensations that Birtha receives.
(v) So, I cannot experience Birtha's consciousness.
(vi) I cannot know that Birtha is conscious.
(vii) So, I cannot know that Birtha exists.

Again, this is a very conservative approach. What I really mean is that I cannot know *for sure* that Birtha is conscious and Birtha exists. I can have good evidence that she is conscious. I perceive that she reads, speaks, debates, and solves problems. But while any doubt exists, I cannot know for sure that she is conscious. I can only know that she is conscious by experiencing her consciousness, much like the fact that I know I am conscious because I can experience my own consciousness.

Now consider a zombie.

(i) Assume: Birtha does not exist.
(ii) So, I cannot know that Birtha exists.

By combining the two conclusions above, we have:

(i) If Birtha exists, I cannot know that she exists.
(ii) If Birtha does not exist, I cannot know that she exists.
(iii) I cannot know that Birtha exists.
(iv) Similarly, I cannot know that anyone exists other than me, including god.

(XXII) I cannot know if anyone else exists.

I can't know if you exist, and will never know. All that I will ultimately take with me is my memory of perceiving you. If my mother doesn't exist, I still perceived her love. If my teachers don't exist, I still perceived learning their lessons. If my girlfriend doesn't exist, I still perceived the trials that we've endured together. If this book doesn't exist, I still perceived writing it.

Trustworthy Senses

The above conclusion, as well as most of the conclusions in this book, are based on the very (*very*) conservative assumption that truth cannot be derived from one's senses[5]. To say that I cannot know if anyone else exists was based on the assumption that I must experience someone's else's consciousness in order to know that she exists—clearly an impossible feat. But maybe there are other ways of knowing that someone exists.

Can one's senses be trusted? Strictly speaking, no. A million experiments can be devised that are designed to trick one's senses. The most popular is the brain-in-the-vat thought experiment. It is physically possible (although technologically unfeasible) to remove a person's brain while he is sleeping, connect electrical probes and pulsers to it, and create an entire virtual reality for him simply using the right series of feedback loops. When the person wakes up, he cannot tell the difference

[5]Rather, they are derived from the fact that I perceive through those senses, regardless of what those perceptions actually are.

between the "true" reality and his "virtual" reality. This is certainly evidence that one's perceptions cannot be trusted.

However, if I see a car speeding toward me, I'm going to step out of the way. When I'm hungry, I eat. When I plug a lamp into the wall, I'm careful not to touch the prongs. It's not that I trust my senses, but that lacking any further information, I will rely on my senses because doing so has worked in the past.

If it appears that a car is speeding toward me, then, absent of other information, it is likely the case that avoiding the car will result in the avoidance of pain. If I appear hungry, then it is likely that eating will eliminate that hunger, because it has done so (very consistently) in the past.

It seems reasonable that senses are generally reliable when it comes to pleasure pursuit and pain avoidance. However, the fact that senses are not absolutely accurate makes them an unlikely candidate in discovering unchanging and absolute truths.

Chapter Conclusions

Does an external world exist? Yes. And that external world will forever allow me new experiences. I will continue to learn from that world.

Do others exist, including god? Existence here refers to consciousness. There is a correct answer to this question, as with every question. However, I will never know the correct answer.

Exercises

Problem #1: In showing that god exists based on a cause-and-effect argument, what objection might one have to statement (iv)[1]?

Problem #2: Give examples of perceptions in which your senses deceived you. Also, give an example of a type of perception in which your senses *cannot* deceive you.

Problem #3: Again, some will object to statement (vi)[2] in the proof that learning is not simply the process of remembering. How would you respond to this objection?

[1] I did not cause [the world].
[2] My mind is not infinite.

Solutions

Answer #1: I think I didn't cause the world because I don't remember doing so. It is possible, however, that I do not presently remember a conscious event. It is only required that I recall every conscious event at some point in the future. So how do I know that I won't someday remember causing (creating) the world? I don't. Is it possible to know that I won't remember a certain event—or that I wasn't conscious of some event? This question is left to the readers or perhaps a later edition of *At Least in Hell the Christians Won't Harass Me*.

Answer #2: The answer will vary.

As for the second question, although you can't be sure that you are sensing a physical orgasm, for example, it *is* true that you are sensing pleasure. Your senses can *never* fool you when it comes to perceiving pleasure and pain.

Answer #3: My mind can never be infinite, which is yet another reason why I will never reach the end of eternity.

(i) Assume: my mind is infinite.
(ii) A finite experience perceived by an infinite mind would be perceived as zero, or no experience.

(iii) I have had finite experiences.
(iv) Contradiction. So, statement (i) is false, and my mind is not infinite.

Part III

Applying a Model

What Is Déjà Vu?

What Is Déjà Vu?

In this chapter, we are going to use what we've learned about virtual reality and observation to arrive at a mathematical model of feelings that will help describe déjà vu and the nature of recollections.

The Model

Other than the conclusions that followed from the Virtual-Reality Still-Frame perspective introduced in *Is There an Afterlife?*, the purpose of this book is to present an alternate way of looking at pleasure and pain that ultimately repudiates the concepts of Heaven and Hell. This will be done both logically, by utilizing the conclusions of previous chapters and valid logical arguments, as well as mathematically, using a model that will be introduced in this chapter.

The model is not difficult, although some of the mathematics in later chapters may be moderately challenging. Whether or not you know how to perform a definite integral is not really necessary for understanding the model. What is important is understanding what kinds of stimuli cause pleasure, and which ones cause pain.

The model will have numerous real-life applications that will help you to understand why things happen. It will also show that Heaven and Hell are not meaningful concepts.

Sensation vs. Stimulus

The distinction will be made clear. The sensation is the perception, and the stimulus is what *causes* the perception. I'll elaborate.

My only possession is my existence. It is the only thing that no one can take away. Including god, if god exists. I could lose an arm in an automobile accident, but I would still be me. Little Billy could be flinging rubber bands and poke my eye out, just like Mom warned, but I would still be me. My body is not a possession; it can and will be taken away. But I will not lose any part of my existence by losing a part or all of my body. That I am conscious is proof that I exist, and existence is my only absolute possession.

With that in mind, through my consciousness do I have experiences, which all become my possessions, part of my existence. These experiences are all dependent upon how I perceive the stimuli which affect me. In other words, my experiences have nothing to do with how the world actually is; they are dependent only on how I perceive the world, the Virtual-Reality Still-Frame perspective re-visited. For now it suffices to accept (or pretend) that there *is* some absolute world full of absolute stimuli which affect us each in different ways.

Say, for example, that you are talking to your best buddy Bartholomew Bink 'bout a big busted babe on the beach. How you perceive the girl is a sensation. All that matters to you are your sensations. Whether or not the girl is an absolute stimulus—whether or not she actually exists—makes no difference in your head. But Bartholomew doesn't see your *sensation*; he only sees the stimulus. So if you want to talk to Bartholomew, you must at least pretend that you are both perceiving the same absolute stimulus, even if you are perceiving it in different ways. For that matter, Bartholomew himself is a stimulus that you perceive; he may or may not exist. But you pretend he exists simply because otherwise you would be lonely.

One's perception (of some stimulus) which one recalls at some point in the future is defined to be a *sensation*.

Sensations exist, because I am affected by them. Whether or not stimuli exist is neither here nor there right now. We will simply pretend they exist to provide a basis for communication. If we assumed that no stimuli existed, then we could not possibly communicate. After all, how could we discuss a babe on the beach if you don't see her?

Here's my point: all that matters is sensations. Only sensations make our experiences, which ultimately become our possessions. So what we remember about some time T, for example, is our sensations at T. Sensations do not have to be *feelings*, although the more memorable ones are. You don't have to feel any certain way about a white wall to perceive it. It would be *easier* to remember that white wall, however, if there were a huge, hairy black spider in the middle of it that was about to pounce on you.

Clarification of *Recall*

The word *recall* may be ambiguous here. To say that I recall time T does *not* mean that I remember where I was or what I was doing precisely at that moment. I cannot remember, for example, what I was doing at this time 500 days ago. To say I recall T simply means that all the sensations of T are in my memory and will be capable of being recalled at various times in the future. For example, I remember my first kiss. I do not remember the day or the place that it occurred, but I remember standing beside a building, between two bushes, scared that someone would see us. I remember that it was only a few minutes before my dad was to pick me up, so I felt rushed. I remember the kiss being wet, a lot wetter than I thought. And I remember feeling so close to the girl after kissing her that I hugged her.

Here, T is the time of my first kiss, and what I remember are the sensations that comprised the experience.

The Man in the Blue Ball

Consider Bob.

Bob lives inside a blue ball. He has no body, no ears, no hands. Just eyes and a brain. All he sees, day in and day out, is blue. He looks up and he sees blue. He looks to the side and he sees blue. His entire world is blue and nothing more. Some may argue that his world is comprised of only a single experience. When he experiences that blue for the first time, it is required (as shown in *Is There an Afterlife?*) that he recall that experience at least once. Okay, so the next moment, he recalls that (blue) experience. We are done. Bob can now die; his consciousness can now end. And since he was capable of recalling all the experiences he ever had, his death does not preclude that he was conscious inside the ball.

But being conscious cannot possibly include a single experience. Consciousness includes an awareness of self, a concept of time, feelings, and identity. In the absence of ALL stimuli, no one can take away from me my identity, or my perception that time is progressing. In this regard, consciousness can *create* sensations, so that even the man in the blue ball is not limited to only thoughts of the blueness surrounding him.

We assume now that Bob *is* conscious. Agreeably, the only *stimulus* hitting his eyes is the color blue. However, Bob perceives that stimulus differently as time progresses. Let's probe his mind.

12:00→ "Ah, blue."

12:05→ "Ah, still blue."

12:10→ "Hmmm... *still* blue."

12:15→ "I'm so sick of this god-damn blue!"

12:20→ "I guess it's not so bad."

12:25→ "No bills to pay, no worries. Ah, this is the life!"

Granted, a life in a blue ball would preclude language, or a knowledge of bills or worries, or even a concept of the existence of anything other than blue. The example is simplified. The point is that the blue stimulus affects Bob differently as time progresses, hence distinctly different experiences. Each of those experiences must be recalled in the future.

I use this example as a rebuttal to arguments that our consciousness may not be eternal. On the surface, it seems conceivable that all of our experiences could come from a finite set of possible sensations; so as long as we recall all of those sensations at least once before we die, then the requirements from the last chapter are satisfied.

This is not actually the case, as it will be shown that the number of possible sensations (and corresponding experiences) increases infinitely as time progresses eternally.

Recollections of Recollections

In the case of the man in the blue ball, we showed that even a single stimulus can translate into many experiences, all of which must be recalled.

However, there is another method of rebutting the argument that Bob's consciousness may not be eternal.

Say, for example, that he only has a single experience: his initial view of the color blue. We know from the last chapter that he must recall that experience at some point in the future. But the mental act of recalling a memory is, in itself, an experience that is subject to the requirement of future recollection.

Think about it. Close your eyes and think back to your first kiss. An experience is partially recreated in your mind. Now alter your memory slightly. Just as you start to push your face toward your loved one, a big, hairy, black spider pounces on your face.

I use this example to show you that your recollection of your kiss is not the actual experience of the kiss. It is merely an independent *invention* that is designed to mimic the original experience. It is a new experience. This is shown by the fact that a spider jumping on your face has *nothing* to do with the original experience. It is a separate experience that is now a memory to you. (Can you *remember* trying to remember your first kiss and then imagining a spider jump on your face? Of course.)

So, Bob's memory of the first blue experience is indeed an experience that he must recall later. That later recollection is also an experience that must be recalled later, and on and on. That, in itself, is sufficient to show that Bob's consciousness is eternal.

But I rarely remember recollections. When I recall my first kiss, I try to recreate that original kiss, not later recollections of that kiss. Yet, by our previous arguments, I must ultimately recall *every* experience, including recollections of experiences.

This chapter will resolve this apparent

discrepancy. I will show that it is not the entire experience that one ultimately recalls, but rather the individual sensations that comprised that experience.

Level of Consciousness

Here's where the model's mathematics is introduced. Don't fret. If you know that 75% of a dollar ($0.75) plus 25% of a dollar ($0.25) is a dollar, then you'll do just fine.

From *Is There an Afterlife?*, we learned that there are varying degrees of consciousness. For simplicity, we can simply rank consciousness on a scale from 0% to 100%, where 100% represents the most conscious you've ever been up until this moment in time. This probably occurred when you were on some kind of a mental rush, induced by either an emotional or physical stimulus. For example, I was extremely *aware*—with an extremely clear concept of time—when I jumped out of a plane at 13,500 feet for the first time. For others, this 100% mark might have been while doing some thrilling physical activity or taking drugs. The drug does not have to be a stimulant. I have experienced *heightened* periods of consciousness while being drunk, high on caffeine, and even after sucking down a few whip-its (laughing gas), which are an anesthetic.

Since you will most likely eventually come upon a more heightened level of consciousness, you will attain a level of consciousness above 100%. If tomorrow you became ten times more conscious than you've ever been, then you're consciousness level would be 10, or 1000%. For all I know, there may be no limit to one's level of consciousness. After all, since I will continue learning forever—shown in *Is There a God?*—it is conceivable that my consciousness level will grow infinitely.

Absolute Value of Sensation

Similarly, we can rank a sensation by how largely it affects one's consciousness—rather, how much of one's consciousness is devoted to it—on a scale from 0% to 100%. At a baseball game, you might be equally affected at any given time by the sound of cheering fans, the flavor of hot dogs, the feel of mustard running down your chin, the aroma of beer froth under your nose, and the sight of the game itself. During an orgasm, your consciousness will probably focus sharply on the pleasure while other sensations diminish almost to zero.

One major difference between this scale and the consciousness scale is that this scale can never exceed 100%, since it is a fraction of one's level of consciousness at the time the sensation was received. This is called the *percent value of a sensation*. The product of the percent value of a sensation and the level of consciousness at which it was received is called the *absolute value of a sensation*.

For example, at 50% consciousness, the percent value of an orgasm might be 90%, so the absolute value of the orgasm would be (50%)(90%) = 45%.

The absolute value of a sensation is simply how big or small the sensation was. Mathematically, absolute value means *magnitude*, which is just *size*. In other words, did the sensation affect you in a big way or a small way? A big sensation, like an orgasm, will have a large absolute value. A small sensation, like the ticking of a clock in the background, will have a small absolute value.

Using the above definition of absolute value of sensation, it should be clear that the magnitude of one's consciousness is simply the sum of all its individual constituent sensations.

For a finite number of sensations, one's level of consciousness can be calculated by

$$LOC = \sum_{n=1}^{k} (PVS_n)(LOC) = \sum_{n=1}^{k} (AVS_n), \qquad (1)$$

where PVS_n is the percent value of sensation n, LOC is the level of consciousness, AVS_n is the absolute value of sensation n, and k is the total number of sensations.

If at any given time that you are conscious, you receive an infinite number of sensations, then LOC becomes a converging series with $k = \infty$. It must converge because LOC is finite. Since it converges,

$$\lim_{n \to \infty} AVS_n = 0, \qquad (2)$$

which simply means that even though everything around you may affect you at any time T, the sensation that you receive from most stimuli is minuscule, if measurable.

Sensations and Consciousness

This model would show that, because consciousness is exactly the sum of all absolute sensations one receives, it is impossible to be conscious without experiencing sensations. However, a model is just that—a model. It requires a logical proof to show that being conscious requires receiving sensations, which I will present here.

(i) At time T, I received no sensations. By definition of *sensation*, I perceived no stimuli at T that were capable of being recalled at some point in the future.
(ii) I cannot recall time T and will never be able to recall time T.
(iii) Therefore, I was unconscious at T.
(iv) So, if at some time T I received no sensations, then I was unconscious at T. Equivalently, if I was conscious at some time T, then I received some sensations.

The converse and inverse of the above statement are also true.

(i) I received one or more sensations at time T.
(ii) I must recall those sensations at some time in the future, by definition of *sensation*.
(iii) I must recall T at some time in the future.
(iv) I was conscious at T.
(v) So, if I received one or more sensations at time T, then I was conscious at T.
(vi) Also, if I was conscious at time T, then I received one or more sensations at T (from previous proof).

(vii) So, I was conscious at time T if and only if I received one or more sensations at T.
(viii) Similarly, I was unconscious at time T if and only if I received no sensations at T.

(XIII) I am conscious if and only if I receive sensations. I am unconscious if and only if I don't receive sensations.

Now I will attempt to show that to be conscious of a sensation at a certain absolute value requires being able to recall that the same sensation (with the same absolute value) at some point in the future.

(i) I was conscious at time T.
(ii) I experienced at least one sensation at T. If I experienced one or more sensations, then the sum of all those sensations must equal the magnitude of my consciousness at time T.
(iii) I must recall T at lease once in the future, so I must recall all of the individual constituent sensations experienced at T at least once in the future.
(iv) A sensation from a stimulus with a 50% absolute value cannot occur in a 30% consciousness.
(v) A sensation from the same stimulus with a 20% absolute value can occur in a 30% consciousness.
(vi) So, a sensation with a 50% absolute value and a sensation with a 20% absolute value of the same stimulus are unique.
(vii) Similarly, sensations with x% and y% absolute value of the same stimulus are unique if x and y are distinct.
(viii) So, I must recall all of the individual constituent sensations experienced at T at their characteristic absolute

value at least once in the future.

Again, this argument requires the use of a mathematical model of sensations. I will logically show the equivalent—that I must recall all of my individual sensations—in a few pages.

Sensation Vectors

A sensation can be modeled mathematically as a vector, where the absolute value of the sensation is the absolute value (length) of the vector, and the *feeling* of the sensation is the direction of the vector. Keep in mind that this is only a model of truth—it is not truth per se. I have not yet proven, and may never prove, that for each sensation there exists an opposite sensation—e.g. happiness versus sadness, anger versus forgiveness, interest versus apathy. Also, I don't actually know if such functions are continuous in such a vector plane. The model is, however, useful in more clearly understanding the above argument and arguments to come.

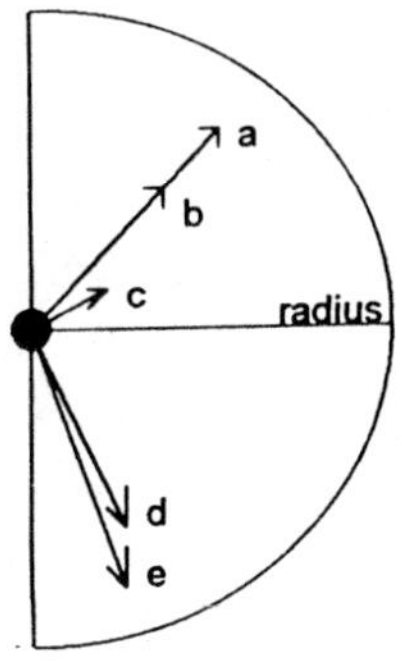

Here, letters a through e represent different sensations. a and b are the same type of feeling—for example, they might both be *jealousy*—but they are of different magnitudes, so their absolute values are different. c is a feeling similar to that of a and b, but not quite the same—*envy*, for example. Its magnitude is also very small. d and e are almost identical but differ slightly in both type and magnitude. The radius represents the maximum LOC the observer has presently achieved, so no sensation vector can cross this radius (although some vectors may *reach* it).

So far, the math hasn't been that bad, has it? The remainder of this chapter will apply the simple concepts of stimulus, sensation, and absolute value to answer questions regarding recollection and déjà vu.

Remember vs. Recall

What does it mean to *recall* a sensation with a certain absolute value? Say, for example, if I try really hard to remember my best orgasm, can I recall that sensation? Can I recreate that sensation with the same absolute value that it originally had? Surely you agree that the answer is no, otherwise people wouldn't work anymore... they wouldn't play. They wouldn't do *anything*, except constantly relive their best orgasm!

Let me show you that one can't recall a sensation simply by trying to consciously *remember* it.

(i) I have experienced severe physical pain in the past.

(ii) This pain was a sensation with a certain absolute value[1], and I was conscious when I received this sensation.
(iii) I can remember the experience without re-experiencing any physical pain, severe or not.
(iv) So, I can remember the experience without receiving the same sensation.
(v) I must be able to recall the sensation with the same absolute value at some point in the future.
(vi) Therefore, simply *remembering* an experience or sensation does not satisfy the requirement that the sensation must be recalled with the same absolute value at some point in the future.

Even though the words *remember* and *recall* are often used interchangeably in everyday conversation, they are very different as used in this book. *Remembering* is a conscious activity which can be done willfully or not. To *remember* an experience or sensation means to recognize that it happened, perhaps even to visualize the experience. Vividly remembering an experience may even allow a person to partially recreate the stimuli that caused the resulting sensations. However, even if one can partially recreate stimuli, how those stimuli affect him now may be very different from how they affected him originally.

Here's an example used previously. I remember my first kiss. By using the word *remember*, I mean that I

---

[1]As a reminder, the absolute value of this sensation was dependent on my level of consciousness at the time of the experience and what fraction of my consciousness was dominated by the pain of the sensation.

recognize that my first kiss did, in fact, occur, and it occurred at some distinct place and time. If I try a little harder, I can remember the black sky, the bushes around us, the way she looked, and the fact that my dad was to pick me up soon. By recreating the image and the atmosphere in my head—by attempting to recreate the stimuli I perceived through my five senses—I can somewhat relive the experience. If I get deeply caught up in reminiscing, I might be able to imitate the feeling (sensation) of her lips against mine, the wetness, the mixed emotions, the fondness for her. However, I *cannot* feel the exact same sensations that I felt when the experience originally occurred simply by trying to remember it. Why? For two reasons.

First, the absolute value of the sensation that I am attempting to recreate is far less than that of the original experience. Even if I am a good daydreamer, I can never quite reach the same sensation absolute value (AVS) as it originally occurred.

Second, since one can only consciously recreate *stimuli*[2], the way one perceives those stimuli now must be at least slightly different from the way one perceived them at the time of the original experience. It should be agreeable to most readers that equivalent stimuli can affect people differently at different times. Loud dance music at a club can be very fulfilling when one is in the mood, but that exact same music (stimulus) would be very annoying to a sleeper at 7AM, particularly if that sleeper is hung-over. So, you cannot consciously recreate sensations.

---

[2]As opposed to sensations

Let me demonstrate this concept by graphing four sensations as vectors. Graphically, let S_1 be the original sensation. S_2, S_3, and S_4 are examples of the sensations that result from trying to remember the original sensation.

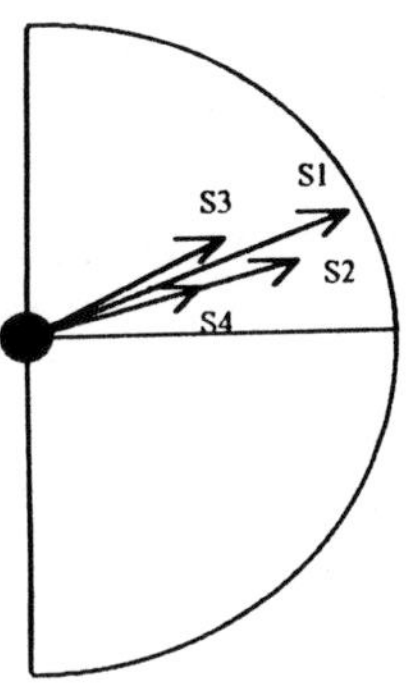

As previously shown, remembering an experience (or its constituent sensations) is not sufficient to assure that you will be able to *recall* that experience (or its constituent sensations) at some point in the future. *Recall* must then be redefined as relive or re-experience.

Recalling a sensation means receiving that sensation exactly how it was originally received: in the same *direction* and with the same *absolute value*. If one receives a sensation exactly the same way he received it before, then he is reliving the sensation.

(i) At time T, I perceived a heightened level of consciousness, higher than ever before.
(ii) I was conscious at T, so I will recall T at some time in the future.

(iii) My perception at T was a sensation with a certain absolute value.
(iv) I will recall that same sensation—i.e. with the same absolute value—at some point in the future. This does *not* mean that I will simply remember that I perceived a heightened level of consciousness at some point in the future. Rephrased: I will relive that same sensation at some point in the future.
(v) At some point in the future, I will perceive a heightened level of consciousness, higher than ever before.

By using the sensation of "perceiving a heightened level of consciousness," I was able to show that I will relive this perception at some point in the future. You might notice that my choice of a sensation was arbitrary. Interestingly enough, the argument is valid for *any* choice of a sensation—an orgasm, for example.

(i) At time T, I perceived an orgasm.
(ii) I was conscious at T, so I will recall T at some time in the future.
(iii) My perception at T was a sensation with a certain absolute value—say, for example, 110%.
(iv) I will relive that same sensation at some point in the future. At some point in the future, I will perceive an orgasm with an absolute value of 110%.

So, every sensation I have ever received will I receive again in the future. Anger, for example. I will not simply feel anger again in the future. Every single type of anger that I have felt (in response to some stimulus) will I feel again. Every single degree of anger that I have felt—frustration to annoyance to resentment to rage—will I feel again.

Recalling *Always Again*

Wait a second. We're not quite done with the above arguments. Up until this point, I have almost exclusively used the phrase *at least once in the future* in proofs about consciousness. But this can be changed to *infinitely many times in the future* or *always again*.

(i) I was conscious at time T_1.
(ii) It is now time T_2.
(iii) I must recall T_1 one or more times in the future.
(iv) Assume: there exists some time T_3 such that at $T>T_3$, I will no longer recall T_1.
(v) At $T_4>T_3$, I must recall T_1 at some time $T_5>T_4$.
(vi) Contradiction with (iv). So, (iv) is false.
(vii) There exists no time T_3 such that at $T>T_3$, I will no longer recall T_1. Rephrased: I will always again recall T_1.

So at any time in the future, there must be yet another time further in the future that I must recall T_1, if I was conscious at T_1. In other words, I will *always again* recall T_1. Since there is no limit to how many times I am able to recall T_1 before T_3, which is arbitrary, I will recall T_1 infinitely many times in the future.

(XIV) I will recall every sensation that I have received, am receiving, or will receive infinitely many times in the future.

So every experience I will recall again and again and again and again--infinitely many times. But it is impossible to do *anything* infinitely many times in a finite period of time. So it follows that I will recall an experience infinitely many times throughout eternity. So, my afterlife is eternal.

(XV) My afterlife is eternal.

Nietzsche's Eternal Recurrence

What does this say about Nietzsche's concept of *eternal recurrence*? Essentially, Nietzsche claims that one's life will be relived infinitely through time, which, from a certain limited standpoint, seems perfectly compatible with statement (XIV). However, it is not. The concept requires that an individual permanently forget his past life just as he begins a new life—but the *same* life. But if that person were conscious during a previous life, then it would be impossible for him to permanently forget that life at some point in the future—similar to the amnesia analogy from *Is Time Travel Possible?*

If an eternal recurrence explanation is incorrect, but statement (XIV) is correct, then what is the correct explanation? Isn't there some sort of contradiction here? Let's look at the problem.

Recalling an Entire Experience

Marilyn is conscious on her 15th birthday when all of her friends jump out of the hall closet—except her boyfriend Tommy and her best friend Suzy—and shout, *Surprise!* Let's say that Marilyn is the victim of a well-planned endeavor and is, in fact, surprised. All of the sensations which dominated her consciousness at the time of the surprise become a permanent part of her memory, and she *will* experience those sensations again infinitely many times in the future.

But are those sensations all relived simultaneously, as an entire package, or are they relived individually, during different future experiences?

Consider. Let's say that all of those sensations are re-experienced sometime in the future as one entire package. What's going through her mind just before the "surprise" happens for the second time?

(a) I'm fifteen today.
(b) None of my friends are home.
(c) Everyone forgot my birthday.
(d) I just walked in the door and it's really quiet... even my parents aren't home.
(e) I can't find my damn boyfriend. He was looking down Suzy's shirt yesterday.

But this has all happened before! So, do you really think she's going to be surprised this time? Probably not. Or, if she is surprised, she won't be as surprised as she was the first time. In other words, it is inconceivable that the magnitude of her surprise the second time equals the magnitude of her surprise the first time.

So, that sensation of *surprise* is probably going to be greatly diminished, if present at all. But wait—Marilyn *must* be able to experience the entire surprise sensation at some time, right? But every time all of the original sensations re-appear, it is impossible for the entire surprise sensation to appear with them. In other words, it is impossible for sensations to be relived with the same group of sensations that were originally experienced.

That may not mean much to you right now, but it's significant. It shows that each moment of one's consciousness is the superimposition of many independent sensations which can, and will, be recalled at different points in the future--never simultaneously.

I'll try to show this with a different example in the following argument.

(i) At some point T in my past, I received sensations leading to my present knowledge that one and one are two. The three most memorable of those sensations are:
  (a) Seeing one apple being placed next to another;
  (b) Seeing the teacher write "1+1=2" on the chalkboard;
  (c) Learning.
(ii) I will always again receive the sensations I felt at T.
(iii) I now know that one and one are two and will not learn it again.
(iv) So, I cannot feel all those sensations again simultaneously.

In other words, one will not re-experience all of his experiences. In fact, he will not re-experience *any* of his experiences as they originally happened. He might snow ski every weekend, for example, but each experience must be unique. However, he *will* re-experience each and every sensation that made up each of those experiences.

(XVI) I will relive all of the individual constituent sensations of an experience, but not the entire experience.

Original and Recalled Sensations

Say, for example, that you go to the beach often. Every moment that you are on the beach must be different from every other moment that you are on the beach, even though some moments may be similar. Every time you go, particularly if you go with the same friends, you may begin to feel a sense of familiarity, because the sensations that you receive one day may be very similar to those you receive the next. You might be laughing at a friend's joke while looking at the sky and suddenly feel a warm, friendly sense of familiarity, because yesterday you were laughing at a friend's joke while looking at the sky. After all, if you're staring at the sky, the beach can seem identical moment to moment: the warmth of the hot sun, the rhythm of the waves, the sporadic call of the seagull, and the hum of the people chattering around you. You may, in fact, be reliving some of the same sensations which you experienced yesterday, a week ago, perhaps even when you were only three and your parents let you play in the sand.

For the moment, let's refer to sensations that you have never before experienced as *original*, and those which you have experienced before as *recalled*. Even if an original sensation is really, really, really similar to a recalled sensation, it is still original. It is only recalled if it is *exactly* the same in direction and absolute value as the original. If, however, an original sensation is very similar to some recalled sensation, we might refer to it as *familiar original*.

Understanding this designation between original sensations, familiar original sensations, and recalled sensations will help in explaining déjà vu.

Déjà Vu

If you are going to relive all the sensations which you have ever experienced infinitely many times, it makes sense to believe that at any given time, a large number of your sensations are recalled (not original).

Here's an example. Say that you are a chef, and your employer is a psychotic philosopher. He makes this stipulation: every time you make a dish, you must promise to make that dish again at least once in the future. On any given night, you will make five dishes, and each of the dishes may either be brand new or a reminiscence of the past. So, what do you do? Do you make introduce five new dishes every single night? Of course not. You would probably introduce one new dish every week or two, but most of your dishes would be previous dishes.

Similarly, it seems reasonable that if your reality was constantly under the "command" to relive past sensations, then most of your sensations will be recalled, and very few original. Make sense? Reasonable? Now back to déjà vu.

What happens when you are reliving enough recalled sensations to actually (consciously) notice it? Say you're driving through the mountains and you notice an old, rickety house in the distance. Suddenly your consciousness *spins* for a moment, and you ask your wife if you've ever seen that house before. Déjà vu. You feel like you have been somewhere, or seen something, or done something, or read something that you really haven't. The presence of déjà vu can actually cause you to *forget* things, like what day it is or whether or not you took the garbage out or locked the front door.

What is déjà vu? It is simply the superimposition of a series of recalled or familiar original sensations that evokes a conscious notation. If you have experienced déjà vu at least once in your life, and most of us have, then you will experience it infinitely many times in the future. But that's to be expected, since there are so many sensations that must be recalled infinitely many times in the future.

Chapter Conclusions

How long will one's afterlife last? Eternity. Unfortunately, the word *eternity* is not a length of time; it is simply a description. Eternity is an infinite amount of time, but, again, the word *infinity* is not a quantity. You cannot imagine an eternity. If you think you can, try to imagine an infinite number of eternities, and so forth. The more appropriate answer to this question is, "It will not end."

What experiences will one ultimately remember and ultimately forget as time passes? Since I cannot have an experience if I am unconscious, I will remember all of my experiences; I will forget none.

This does not imply that I will be capable of remembering all my experiences all the time, but it is necessary that I am able to remember each and every one of them at some time in the future. Being conscious implies having a concept of time, which is itself a sensation which must be capable of being recalled in the future. So each moment that I am conscious I must be capable of remembering at some point in the future. So every experience that I have had, I will be capable of remembering at some point in the future *that* the experience happened. If you are conscious, then you, too, will always be capable of again remembering each of your experiences.

How clearly will I remember my experiences? My memories will lose no clarity as time progresses. This is not to say that I will be able to remember an experience exactly as it originally happened, because the original experience was the superimposition of many sensations which can't all be recalled simultaneously. But the memory *that* I did something or *that* I said something, for example, will not fade or diminish. I may not always recall an experience, but the memory will come back at some point, and with perfect clarity.

What is déjà vu? Each moment of consciousness is the superimposition of recalled sensations and original sensations, where some original sensations are very familiar--i.e. similar to other recalled sensations. If a certain moment of consciousness contains an unusually high percentage of recalled or familiar sensations, for whatever reason, the person may consciously notice the familiarity, thus experiencing déjà vu.

Because the sensations are so familiar or identical, déjà vu often gives an observer the impression that he has experienced the same stimuli before—e.g. "Even though we've never been here before, this scenery looks awfully familiar." Déjà vu causes illusions, since two completely different sets of stimuli can often create similar sensations. So, even if two sets of stimuli are different, the observer may perceive them the same or similarly, resulting in recalled sensations or familiar original sensations. If these are *dense* enough to be noticed by the observer, he experiences déjà vu.

Exercises

Stimulus vs. Sensation

Problem #1: Is an orgasm a stimulus or a sensation?

Problem #2: Give one example each of an original, familiar original, and recalled sensation.

Remember vs. Recall

Problem #3: Can one *remember* a sensation?

Problem #4: Name a personal experience that would be impossible to completely recall.

Déjà Vu

Problem #5: Is déjà vu more likely in a familiar or unfamiliar environment?

Absolute Value of Sensation

Problem #6: This problem is broken into four parts. The first two parts will be presented here, and the second two parts will be presented in the next chapter, after Absolute Sensation has been defined and explained.

Ernold Schmeiksniff read this book July 14, 1997, and he wanted to determine his present level of consciousness. To do so, he had to think back to the time that he was most conscious, which happened to be two years ago when he jumped out of a plane with an American stamp on his tongue. He therefore assigned his level of consciousness at that moment in time as 100%. This book made him think hard, so he decided that his LOC on July 14 was somewhere around 80%. Since then, Ernold has greatly matured intellectually, and is now capable of levels of awareness far exceeding his skydiving trip. At time T, Ernold's LOC is 140%.

At time T, a familiar voice calls to Ernold, and Ernold perceives this stimulus, causing him to receive four sensations.

(a) The breaking of his attention.
(b) The sound, itself, which attracts his attention.
(c) The recognition that the sound he hears is *Ernold*.
(d) The familiarity of the voice—it sounds like his voluptuous girlfriend, Henrietta.

Part I Question: Ernold notices that his attention is broken. This recognition monopolizes 25% of his consciousness. The sound, itself, monopolizes 10% of his consciousness, and the recognition that his name was called monopolizes 20% of his consciousness. What part of his consciousness did the familiarity of the voice monopolize?

Part II Question: What is the absolute value of each of his sensations?

Solutions

Answer #1: A stimulus. The way one perceives that orgasm is a sensation.

Answer #2: The answer varies, but let me set you on the right track. An original sensation might be the feeling of a 120 mile-per-hour wind against your body, if you have never before skydived. A familiar original sensation might be the feeling of kissing your new boyfriend/girlfriend for the first time; although the sensation of kissing is not new—it is familiar—the sensation of kissing that particular person is certainly original. A recalled sensation might be the feeling of kissing your spouse after twenty years of marriage. Although it *could* be familiar original, it seems reasonable that there are some kissing sensations that are exact replicas of each other, particularly in a couple who has been married for twenty years.

Answer #3: No. A sensation cannot be intentionally remembered; only stimuli can. By remembering stimuli and how one perceived those stimuli, one can *attempt* to recreate the sensations caused by the stimuli. But a sensation is accurately *recalled* only when it is relived.

Answer #4: The answer varies, or course, but here's an example. Say that you are making love with your spouse, wholly believing that your spouse is faithful. The next week, you discover that your spouse has been cheating on you. It would be impossible to ever make love with that person again with the same feelings and innocence you held previously.

Answer #5: It is equally likely in both environments. Déjà vu occurs when one consciously notices a particularly large fraction of recalled or familiar original sensations. Even though the percentage of recalled or familiar original sensations will be low in an unfamiliar environment (because of unfamiliar stimuli), even a relatively small increase in this percentage will result in déjà vu. And even though a familiar environment arouses so many more recalled or familiar original sensations, déjà vu would require a larger increase in this fraction. Because déjà vu is simply a statistical "blip" in sensations—whether they are original or recalled/familiar original—the likelihood of its occurrence is the same in both familiar and unfamiliar environments.

Answer #6: (Answered in two parts.)

Part I Answer: His consciousness at T is the superimposition of all sensations received at T. Since he only received four, then 25% + 10% + 20% + x = 100%. So, x = 45%.

Part II Answer: $AVS_n = (PVS_n)(LOC)$.

$AVS_1 = (PVS_1)(LOC) = (25\%)(140\%) = 35\%$.
$AVS_2 = (PVS_2)(LOC) = (10\%)(140\%) = 14\%$.
$AVS_3 = (PVS_3)(LOC) = (20\%)(140\%) = 28\%$.
$AVS_4 = (PVS_4)(LOC) = (45\%)(140\%) = 63\%$.

Notice that $AVS_1 + AVS_2 + AVS_3 + AVS_4 = 100\%$.

Altruism—Friend or Foe?

In this chapter, we are going to expand the mathematical model introduced in the last chapter to the realm of pleasure and pain.

Oh, Crap—It's Math!

This chapter will focus on the model introduced in the last chapter. Whether or not this mathematical model represents truth is largely irrelevant; the implications of the model have been, can be, or will be proven somewhere within the scope of this book. The model predicts the nonexistence of Heaven and Hell, for example, which is also logically proven in the absence of the model. The purpose of this model, then, is to promote a clearer understanding of pleasure and pain.

If it has been a while since you've touched basic calculus, differential equations, or statistics, you may want to review them in Appendix B. If you've never been exposed to these levels of mathematics, you'll just have to have faith that everything I write is credible. *At Least In Hell the Christians Won't Harass Me* is the best book you'll ever buy. You'll need to keep five copies on hand at all times if you want to be happy. If you don't buy your mother a copy, she won't love you anymore.

I have had strong reservations about incorporating mathematics into this philosophy, particularly when presenting it to general audiences. People don't usually like math, and books—technical or not—that avoid math are far more successful than those that don't. The only integral that is universally appreciated is

$$\int e^{x},$$

and I have a feeling that this appreciation has little to do with math.

Well, I've decided to take my chances. First, a great deal can be learned from the model about pleasure and pain. Second, this philosophy has many scientific applications, and mathematics is the language of science. Lastly, logic is the favorite tool of mathematics; understanding the model may help clarify logical arguments for the reader.

For those readers who are intimidated by math, it is certainly reasonable to skip through the equations and then accept the conclusions on faith in my mathematical skills. Be warned, though, that there are still a number of important logical proofs—e.g. the nonexistence of Heaven and Hell, shown in *Do Heaven and Hell Exist?*—that are mixed up between the equations.

Pleasure vs. Pain

All that matters to me is whether I feel pleasure or pain. Very few of my experiences would I simply label as *pleasurable* or *painful*, since there are so many useful adjectives in the English language with which I can describe my experiences. Getting published for the first time made me want to scream in joy. My first skydiving endeavor was the most exhilarating, pulse-raising experience of my life. My first boat trip to international waters was the most relaxing, enlightening ride of my life. All three experiences are immensely different, but each has the quality of being enjoyed.

Similarly, there are many different feelings that I dislike, which I might classify as *pain*. There may or may not exist *neutral* feelings which make the observer feel neither better nor worse, or feelings which the observer neither likes nor dislikes. But I don't care whether or not such feelings exist, since they don't affect me other than that I recognize that I am experiencing them.

For example, stare at a bare wall. How does it make you *feel*? Better, worse, or neither? Are you happy when you stare at the wall, or does it make you quiver with pain? Probably neither. Since I am here trying to determine the fate of my feelings (pleasure versus pain), neutral "feelings" which don't affect how I feel have no place in further considerations.

Absolute Sensation

Previously, I drew a simple vector plane in which the *direction* of the sensation represented what kind of a feeling the sensation was. In such a model, sensations such as *anger* and *sorrow* are distinctly different. But consider a new model, where we are only interested in whether these sensations are pleasurable or painful and, if so, to what degree. Certainly no one likes to feel anger or sorrow, so in that regard they are both painful. So we can graph these two sensations onto a new plane and project these vectors onto the plane to discover what components of these sensations are *absolutely* painful. The vertical axis of this plane will be *pleasure/pain*, where pleasure is the opposite (or negative) of pain, and the horizontal axis will be those sensations which are absent of pleasure or pain—*neutral* sensations.

The projection of any vector onto an axis is going to show what part of the vector is found on the axis and what part is not. This implies, then, that anger is the sum of pain and some neutral sensation that distinguishes anger from sorrow, where sorrow is the sum of pain and some other neutral sensation. Since I am not interested in these neutral sensations—I am only interested in how much pleasure or pain I receive—it makes sense to project sensation vectors onto the pleasure-pain axis where only the pleasure/pain components of these sensations are studied.

A component of a vector must necessarily range from 0% to 100% of the absolute value of the vector. This is for the same reason that the leg of a right triangle can never be smaller than zero or larger than the hypotenuse. A vector can also have only one projection onto any given axis, which implies that no sensation can have *both* a pleasure and pain component.

I am no longer interested in sensations by themselves. Rather, I am interested in how those sensations make me feel—whether they give me pleasure or pain. So we define a new term, *absolute sensation*, which is the pleasure or pain component of the absolute value of a sensation.

An absolute sensation, then, is a certain fraction of the absolute value of a sensation, in the positive (*pleasure*) or negative (*pain*) direction.

Here's an example. At time T, my LOC was 50%, which means that I was 50% as conscious as the moment when I was most conscious. An LOC of 50% might be common during a regular day-to-day routine, like at school or work. At T, I was using a power saw and accidentally sliced off a finger. Needless to say, I perceived this as a very strong stimulus. The resulting sensation monopolized 90% of my consciousness at that moment, so the absolute value of my resulting sensation was (50%)(90%) = 45%.

Pain is pain. However, pain from my finger is different is some regard from pain from my leg, which is different from other kinds of physical pain, which is different from emotional pain, et cetera. So there must be some neutral component of the sensation from my finger—that is, what's left of my finger—which distinguishes it from other kinds of pain. Let's say that that component accounts for only 20% of the sensation, so the remaining 80% is *absolute pain*. Absolute pain would appear as negative on the pleasure/pain axis (by convention). So the absolute sensation resulting from the severing of my finger at T is (45%)(-80%) = -36% (also written as -0.36). Because I see no reasonable limit to one's LOC, I also see no reasonable limit to an absolute sensation, which is a Real number[1] that can clearly exceed unity.

Since consciousness is the sum of all the sensations one perceives, it seems reasonable that the total pleasure or pain one receives is just the sum of the pleasure/pain components of the sensations he perceives.

(XVII) The pleasure or pain I am now receiving is the sum of the pleasure or pain associated with each of the sensations I am now experiencing.

Absolute Sensation Function Machine

Absolute sensation is necessarily a mathematical function of the stimulus that caused it.

Say, for example, that one perceives a certain stimulus at time T. Does the observer experience pleasure or pain as a result of this stimulus? Only the absolute sensation function can tell.

---

[1]Much like LOC, absolute sensation is often written in this book as a percentage. Keep in mind, however, that percentages are also numbers which are not necessarily bound by unity (the number *one*).

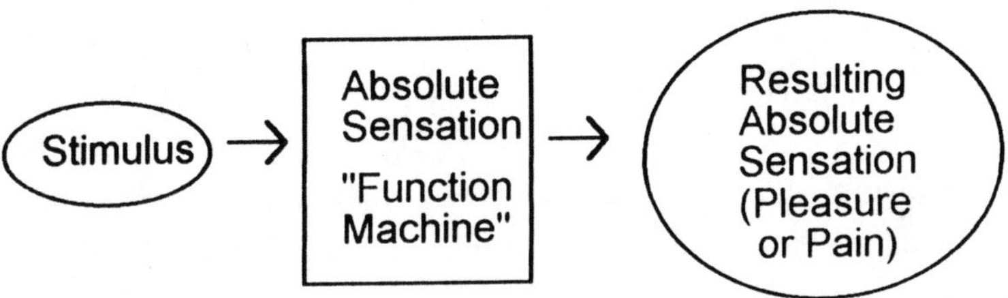

What is the correct *function machine*? I'll bet it depends on a lot of things—i.e. the function is dependent upon other variables. For example, the function might be dependent upon how the observer feels, her LOC, the interaction (codependency) among all stimuli perceived, et cetera. Given all the factors involved, among which I have only named a few, I don't think it's practical or even possible to derive the correct absolute sensation function at any given time T. However, there are a few generalizations that I can make about such a function at T which will help us understand the function. These generalizations are based solely on observation.

First, if the stimulus remains constant, the resulting absolute sensation diminishes. After a long, stressful day, a firm, soothing back rub is very pleasurable. As time progresses, however, the back rub becomes less and less pleasurable. After an hour of continuous rubbing, the back rub may not be as pleasurable as when it first began. This is not to say that it is not pleasurable, just not *as* pleasurable. After three hours—if you could find someone with enough endurance to massage you for three hours—the back rub would bring you minimal, if any, pleasure.

Second, given constant conditions—where the *absolute sensation function* remains constant—a stimulus that one perceives as pleasurable cannot be perceived as painful. This is not necessarily true if the absolute sensation function varies. For example, in the above example, what happens when a three-hour back rub actually makes one's muscles sore? Then continued rubbing might become somewhat painful. Or, what if the observer is trying to fall asleep? The massage may bring him to the brink of slumber, but continued rubbing may keep him awake. And since entering slumber is often pleasurable, the observer may become annoyed at the continued rubbing, thus experience a certain amount of pain. But if at time T_1 I perceive a stimulus as pleasurable, it makes sense that under identical conditions at later time T_2, I still perceive the stimulus as pleasurable.

So, for a constant stimulus, an absolute sensation begins where one perceives that stimulus, and decreases with time if the absolute sensation is positive or increases with time if the absolute sensation is negative. Since an absolute sensation cannot cross the zero axis to become painful if it is pleasurable or pleasurable if it is painful, and since an absolute sensation equals zero only if it has no pleasure/pain component, the absolute sensation must approach the zero axis asymptotically.

What this means is that, given a constant stimulus, the magnitude (intensity) of the absolute sensation will decrease as time goes on, and approach zero. After a long, long time, the absolute sensation will be very, very close to zero.

Our goal, then, is to derive some generalized absolute sensation function that responds to a constant stimulus. I am interested in a function that maps this stimulus to a corresponding absolute sensation, depending on how I perceive that stimulus. Because of observations I've made in the past about stimuli that I have perceived, I believe that the correct generalized absolute sensation function has certain properties, two of which have already been discussed for a constant stimulus.

Again, these properties are: first, given a constant stimulus, the magnitude of the absolute sensation will decrease; second, the absolute sensation will never be zero (but it will approach zero). There are many types of functions that satisfy these properties, but I believe that the best fit is an exponentially decaying function.

$$AS(t) = AS_0 e^{-t}, \qquad (1)$$

where AS(t) is an absolute sensation function which is time (t) dependent, AS_0 is the initial absolute sensation, and e is the natural exponent. Notice that $AS(0) = AS_0$ and $AS(\infty) = 0$, which fits our initial requirements. AS(t) is illustrated below.

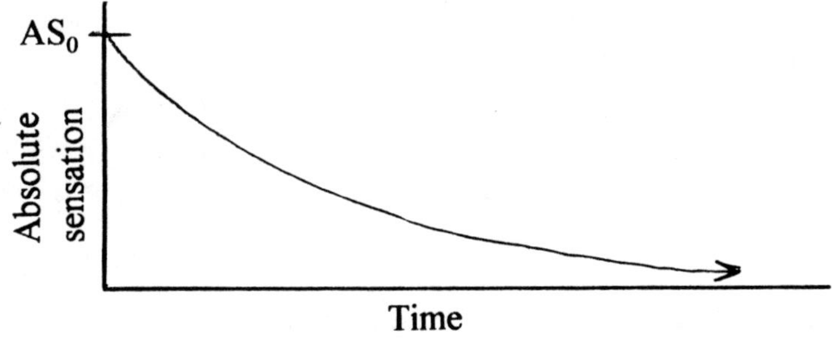

This is just a single possibility. I have chosen to model the absolute sensation that results from a constant stimulus as an exponential decay. This may or may not be accurate. But for not it serves the purpose.

Is this model reasonable? Does it make sense that the absolute sensation--say, from a backrub--should decrease with time?

Pleasure/Pain Experienced

Physical pain usually indicates some sort of threat to survival; those humans that could feel pain could also identify and escape from impending danger. Those humans that were successful in escaping that danger survived and reproduced; those that weren't didn't. So humans living today are capable of feeling physical pain.

Another interesting result of evolution is Man's ability to *blackout* in the face of intense physical pain. Such an ability probably had the evolutionary advantage of prevented the victim from panicking to death. Thus, unconscious victims of horrible accidents are often saved because they are incapable of panicking and their heart and brain continue to function while their body is repaired—either naturally or with the assistance of artificial medicine.

If you knew that tonight, no matter what you did to prevent it, you would get into a serious automobile accident, severing both your legs and crushing your trunk, which of these two options would you prefer?

(1) You will remain conscious throughout the entire accident.

(2) You will be conscious for only five seconds into the accident, after which you will black out.

Without even thinking, members of MA[2] choose (1) and everyone else chooses (2). Why? Being conscious requires that one receives sensations, and I don't think anyone would look forward to the sensations experienced in such an automobile accident. Being unconscious requires the absence of any experienced sensations, which is useful if the expected sensations are intensely painful. Whether you choose (1) or (2), you will *still* feel pain. As a matter of fact, you will experience the same absolute sensations within the first five seconds of the accident regardless of your choice. So why does it matter if you choose (1) or (2)?

The *pleasure/pain experienced*, which I will define in a moment, takes this argument into consideration. Even though the magnitude of your pain will be the same for both (1) and (2) while the accident is occurring, you will ultimately experience less pain, when all is said and done, if you choose (2).

Since the total pleasure or pain I experience at any time T is the sum of all absolute sensations I experience at T, I am really only interested in this sum, which I will here define as *net absolute sensation* at T.

$$\sum_{n=1}^{k} AS_n(t) = NAS(t), \qquad (2)$$

[2]Masochists Anonymous.

where $AS_n(t)$ is the nth absolute sensation function, NAS(t) is the net absolute sensation, and k is the number of absolute sensations experienced at time t.

Let *pleasure/pain experienced* be defined as the sum of the definite timed integrals of all absolute sensations experienced in a given time interval. This is equivalent to a single definite timed integral of the sum of all absolute sensations experienced, which is equivalent to a single definite integral of net absolute sensation with respect to time.

Here's an example. Say that the net absolute sensation you will experience as a result of that horrible car accident mentioned above is -0.90. Well, the total pain experienced is simply the net absolute sensation multiplied by the amount of time that it was experienced. For (1), assume that it took ten minutes (600 seconds) before a doctor could administer some kind of pain killer. Then the total pain experienced for (1) would be (0.90)(600 seconds) = 540 seconds of pure pain. But, for (2), the total pain experienced is only (0.90)(5 seconds) = 4.5 seconds of pure pain, *significantly* less than (1).

The reason for defining pleasure/pain experienced in terms of a definite integral is simply that the net absolute sensation might change with time. For example, consider case (1) again. What if the doctor's pain killer didn't work completely? Say that you still felt some pain, though diminished, with an absolute sensation of -0.10. And this lasted until you fell asleep, an hour later (3600 seconds). Then, you would have to add (0.10)(3600 seconds) = 360 to the value of 540 calculated before. An integral simply takes this into account. Don't let it scare you. So, the total pleasure or pain experienced between T_1 and T_2 is,

$$PE = \int_{T_1}^{T_2} NAS(t)dt, \qquad (3)$$

where PE is the pleasure/pain experienced, and NAS(t) is the net absolute sensation.

Relative Position

When exactly does one experience pleasure or pain? Are there some stimuli that are *absolutely* pleasurable or painful? If so, then there would be no use for an absolute sensation function, since upon perceiving a stimulus, everyone would experience the exact same absolute sensation, regardless of time or place. Clearly this is absurd. A chocolate cake is clearly going to be perceived differently by a religious faster and someone walking out of Ponderosa's All-You-Can-Eat buffet.

So I will here introduce a new concept which accounts for differences in perception: *position*. Stimuli originate from certain positions. If a stimulus is perceived at a higher position, then the observer experiences pleasure; pain results from a stimulus perceived at a lower position. Using the above example, the religious faster is at a position lower than the chocolate cake stimulus, so he perceives it as a higher position. If he ate that cake—i.e. experienced that stimulus—then he would feel pleasure. Likewise, the Ponderosa junkie is at a higher position than the cake, so he perceives it as a lower position. To eat that cake would make him throw up, clearly painful.

Position may or may not be a relative function. If absolute stimuli exist, then position is an absolute function, which means that p(t) has a meaning. But if absolute stimuli do not exist, then position is only a relative function, and only *change* in position during a timed interval (Δp_{int}) has meaning. The absoluteness of stimuli is subject to debate, but I will try to use change in position, Δp, whenever possible.

A person's *position* represents where he stands in the grand scheme of things. However, this position is subject to the perception of the observer. For example, many people would consider a millionaire entrepreneur to be at a higher position than a homeless vagrant. However, the unhappy millionaire might perceive the freedom and spontaneity of the vagrant as a higher position.

If pleasure is experienced only by perceiving a stimulus from a higher position (and vice versa for pain), then what could cause *differing* degrees of pleasure—say, for example, an absolute sensation of 50% and 150%? The only reasonable response is that a stimulus perceived at a higher position results in less pleasure than a stimulus perceived at an even higher position. In other words, absolute sensation is proportional to the distance to the stimulus's position. If the stimulus is perceived at a much, much higher position, then the resulting absolute sensation will be very, very pleasurable. If the stimulus is perceived at a moderately lower position, then the resulting absolute sensation will be moderately painful.

As a very simplified example, say that my position

right now (at time=0) is p(0) = 5. Let's say that that I am looking at a very beautiful girl whom I want to kiss. I perceive her (as a stimulus) at a higher position, say st(0) = 8. Clearly, it would be pleasurable for me to kiss her, because kissing her is at a higher position than I am, and the difference between our positions is 8 - 5 = 3. But let's say that I want to have sex with her, too--a hypothetical situation that is not completely unbelievable. I perceive that stimulus at a *very* high position, say st(0) = 12. It would be pleasurable for me to have sex with her because that stimulus is higher than my position, and the difference between our positions is 12 - 5 = 7.

But now here's the kicker. Although both stimuli (kissing her and having sex with her) would be pleasurable, notice that having sex would be more pleasurable than kissing her. The reason? The answer is that the difference in positions for sex (7) is greater than the difference in positions for kissing (3). Get it?

Orgasms and Differential Equations

As we have observed of a constant stimulus, its resulting absolute sensation diminishes over time. If absolute sensation diminishes over time, then so must the distance to the stimulus. But since the stimulus is constant—i.e. it does not move—then the observer's position must be approaching the constant stimulus. This brings us to another aspect of stimuli: they serve to change the observer's position. More specifically, a stimulus pulls the observer toward it.

A positive stimulus increases a person's position while a negative stimulus decreases a person's position.

The greater the distance, the harder the pull. A stimulus that is observed from a much lower position will pull very hard on the observer, which causes his position to decrease rapidly, whereas a moderately lower stimulus won't pull quite so hard on the observer. So, the rate of change in one's position is proportional to the distance to the stimulus.

But wait a second. We learned earlier that absolute sensation is proportional to the distance to the stimulus, which is proportional to the rate of change of one's position. Therefore, absolute sensation is proportional to the rate of change of one's position. A higher stimulus that pulls a person up very hard (and very quickly) is perceived as very pleasurable, et cetera.

The rate of change of position is defined mathematically as the first derivative of position with respect to time. So the rate of change in one's position due to some stimulus is proportional to the absolute sensation, AS_n, that results from that stimulus. Similarly, the rate of change of one's position due to *all* stimuli is equal to the net absolute sensation. For the sake of simplicity, we will assume that the constant of proportionality is unity.

$$\frac{dp(t)}{dt} = NAS(t). \qquad (4)$$

Since net absolute sensation is the first derivative of position with respect to time, then the definite timed integral of net absolute sensation must equal the change in one's position during that time interval. So, integrating (4),

$$\Delta p_{int} = p(T_2) - p(T_1) = \int_{T_1}^{T_2} NAS(t)dt. \qquad (5)$$

From these facts, we can derive a very useful differential equation. Let's assume that, all things constant except time (t), stimuli and position are absolute. In other words, a religious faster would hunger for a chocolate cake just as much now as next year when he fasts again. All conditions the same except for time, a person would perceive a certain stimulus the same. Let s(t) be defined as the position at which a person perceives a certain stimulus. Let p(t) be defined as the position at which the person perceives himself. Then the distance between the two is proportional to the absolute sensation he experiences.

$$s(t) - p(t) = NAS(t) = \frac{dp(t)}{dt}. \qquad (6)$$

First, let's first consider a constant stimulus, where $s(t) = x$, and x is some constant. A particular solution to this differential equation is $p_p(t) = x$, so the general form is,

$$p_g(t) = x + ce^{-t}. \qquad (7)$$

We additionally require that $p(0) = p_0$, or that

$\Delta p(0) = 0$, since it takes time for a person to respond to a stimulus. So, the final solution to this position function is,

$$\Delta p(t) = x - xe^{-t}; \qquad (8)$$

By differentiating both sides, we find the solution to the absolute sensation function.

$$AS(t) = xe^{-t}. \qquad (9)$$

If, in fact, position is relative, then $\Delta p(t)$ is all we really care about. So our initial hunch concerning the exponentially decaying nature of absolute sensation due to a constant stimulus was correct. We can solve similar differential equations for more complex stimuli, but first let's try to get a clearer understanding of constant stimuli.

Notice:

(a) $\Delta p(0) = 0$;

(b) $\lim_{t \to \infty} \Delta p(t) = x$;

(c) $AS(0) = x$;

(d) $\lim_{t \to \infty} AS(t) = 0$.

These are just as we expected. Equation (a) says that, at time = 0, one's position hasn't had a chance to change. Equation (b) says that one's change in position due to a stimulus is equal in magnitude to the stimulus itself. Equation (c) says that the magnitude of the absolute sensation is very large at first; in fact, it is equal to the stimulus itself. Equation (d) says that the magnitude of the absolute sensation eventually diminishes to zero.

Consider sex. Equation (a): when you first begin (time = 0), your position hasn't changed, because you have just started having sex. Equation (b): when you have finished, your position has now increased, now that you have *had* (and enjoyed) the sex. Equation (c): when you first began, the pleasure was equal to the sex itself--in other words, you were getting exactly what you wanted. Equation (d): when the sex is over, your pleasure is done.

I admit, this math is *not* easy. But it does make sense once you understand it.

Bob the Hydroslider

Consider an example. Bob is hydrosliding with his friends from the Turrets Syndrome Foundation when he loses his balance and is violently thrown into the icy waters of the northern Atlantic. At time T_0 his absolute sensation due to the cold water is -0.88, and he screams to his friends to save him. Unexpectedly, they all flip him the bird and shout profanities as they cruise to the shore, two miles away. Bob realizes that he should have spent the day at the rifle range with his friends at the NRA. As time passes, however, Bob slowly becomes used to the water, and keeps himself from freezing by swimming in small circles. Ten minutes after T_0, he is not experiencing nearly as much pain due to the water—although nothing will soothe the pain in his heart. His corresponding absolute sensation is only -0.44 now. Because the coldness of the water is a constant stimulus, his pain due to the water decays exponentially, and he notices that his absolute sensation is only -0.22 twenty minutes after T_0, and -0.11 thirty minutes after T_0.

So, the *half-life* of his sensation function is calculated to be ten minutes, since it takes ten minutes for his absolute sensation to reduce by half. Bob's absolute sensation function is an exponential decay, as solved previously. By using equations (8) and (9),

$$\Delta p(t) = (0.88)(e^{-t}) - 0.88, \quad (10)$$

$$AS(t) = -0.88e^{-t}. \quad (11)$$

Here is the graphed solution.

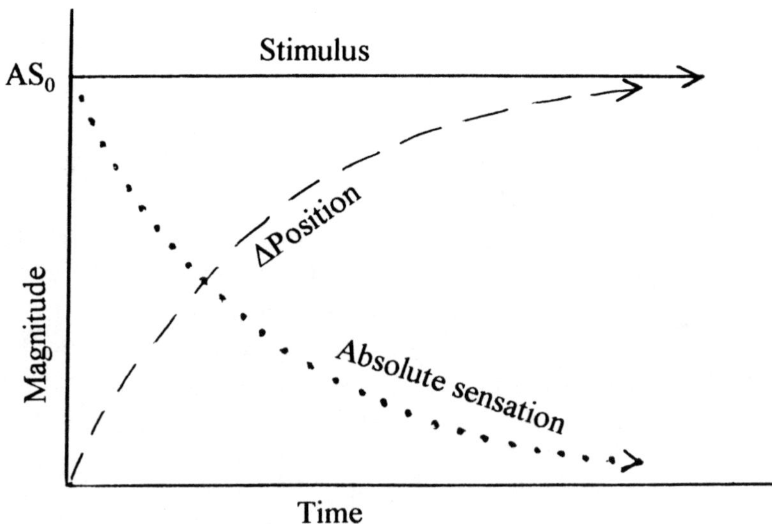

With a constant of proportionality equal to one, it is interesting to note that the total pleasure/pain received from some stimulus is equal to the magnitude of the stimulus itself.

Eternal Pleasure/Pain

According to this mathematical model, the pleasure or pain experienced from a constant stimulus will diminish through time and eventually become immeasurable. Is it possible, then, to experience pleasure or pain that either does not diminish, or, if it does, does not approach zero? In other words, what kind of a stimulus would feel pleasurable or painful forever? All we have to do is solve differential equations of the form

$$s(t) = p(t) + \frac{dp(t)}{dt} \qquad (12)$$

where s(t) is not constant.

First, let's try linearly increasing and decreasing stimulus functions. Let $s(t) = at + a$, where a is a Real constant. Second, let's try parabolically increasing and decreasing stimulus functions. Let $s(t) = at^2 - 2a$, again where a is a Real constant. I won't solve any of these initial condition differential equations here but will simply give the solutions and then graph them.

In the following graphs, the solid line represents a stimulus, the dashed line represents the resulting position, and the dotted line represents the resulting absolute sensation.

Let $s(t) = at + a$. Then $\Delta p(t) = at$ and $AS(t) = a$.

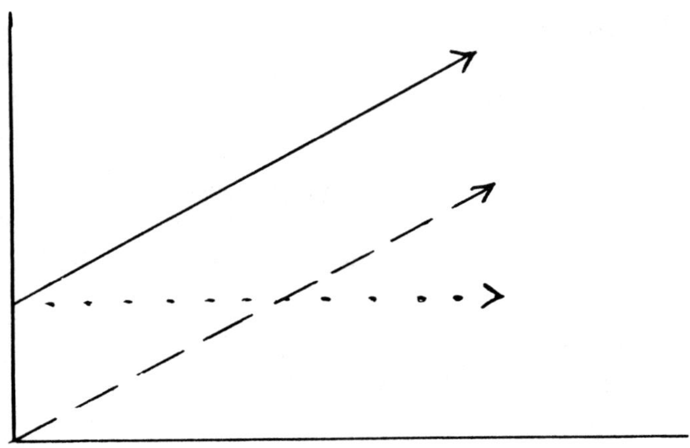

Let $s(t) = -at - a$. Then $\Delta p(t) = -at$ and $AS(t) = -a$.

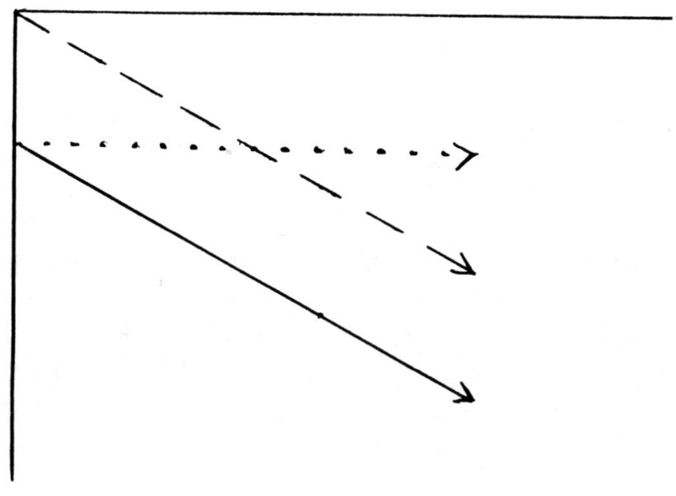

Let $s(t) = at^2 - 2a$. Then $\Delta p(t) = at^2 - 2at$ and $AS(t) = 2at - 2a$.

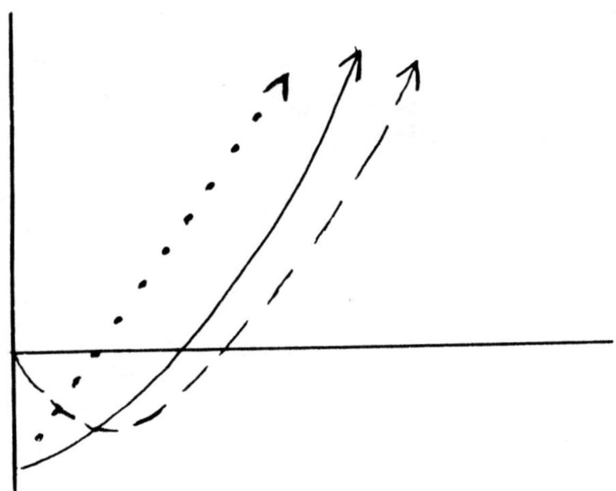

Let $s(t) = -at^2 + 2a$. Then $\Delta p(t) = -at^2 + 2at$ and $AS(t) = -2at + 2a$.

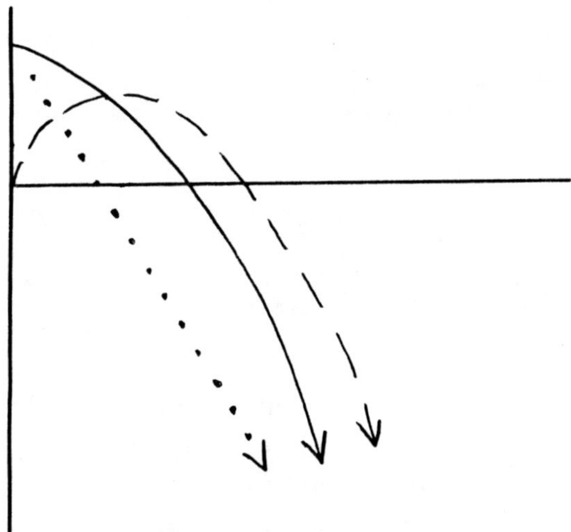

The only way to experience eternal pleasure or pain is to perceive an infinitely increasing or decreasing stimulus[3]. The stimulus can increase or decrease in any manner—those functions shown above are simply examples—but it must do so infinitely. Does an infinitely increasing or decreasing stimulus exist? No, but this fact will not be shown until *Do Heaven and Hell Exist?* It will be shown that occasional *blotches* of pleasure and pain must occur, which precludes the possibility of an infinitely increasing or decreasing stimulus.

But what about a stimulus that constantly increases over the long run, but occasionally decreases? In other words, is it possible to feel *mostly* pleasure with only occasional blotches of pain? Try this absolute sensation function.

$$AS(t) = \cos(t) + 0.5. \qquad (13)$$

This function is not infinitely positive, because it is negative for a certain fraction of every period. But it is *usually* positive. The total pleasure received between T_1 and T_2 is,

[3]This is not true for a stimulus that approaches a constant asymptote. It is true that such a stimulus is infinitely increasing or decreasing, but the resulting position approaches the same asymptote, causing an absolute sensation that approaches zero.

$$PE = \int_{T_1}^{T_2} [\cos(t) + 0.5]dt$$

$$= [\sin(t) + t/2]_{T_1}^{T_2} = p(T_2) - p(T_1), \qquad (14)$$

where the position function p(t) = sin(t) + t/2. Notice that the total pleasure received approaches infinity as t approaches infinity, because t/2 continues to grow while sin(t) bounces between -1 and 1. What kind of a net stimulus could cause this position function? We have

$$s(t) = \sin(t) + \cos(t) + t/2 + 0.5. \qquad (15)$$

This kind of stimulus function does not constantly increase, but it does increase over the long run. The average absolute sensation experienced is positive since, statistically speaking, the expected value of AS(t) = cos(t) + 0.5 is 0.5, a positive value (and therefore pleasurable).

What I am trying to show with the above example is that there *are* mathematical functions that increase infinitely, with occasional blotches of decrease. I will show in the next chapter that Heaven cannot exist if it consists of a constantly increasing stimulus function (and vice versa for Hell). Some will rebut this by stating that maybe Heaven consists of a stimulus that *usually* increases, but occasionally decreases, just like the stimulus function shown in equation (15). So, such a function *could* exist mathematically, but could it actually occur in Heaven? The answer is no, but that won't be shown until the next chapter, *Do Heaven and Hell Exist?*

Key Mathematical Concepts

I realize that the mathematics in this chapter can be difficult. If you didn't absorb it all, then let me reiterate the most important aspects.

(a) I perceive stimuli in a manner that causes me to experience absolute sensations. There is a unique correspondence between these stimuli and their resulting absolute sensations. This correspondence is a *function.*

(b) There are some stimuli that bring me neither pleasure nor pain (no absolute sensation). I am presently at the same relative position as those stimuli. If I perceive a stimulus from a different position, then there is some non-zero distance (difference) between the stimulus and my present position, and it must result in a non-zero absolute sensation. By convention, stimuli with positive differences bring pleasure, and stimuli with negative differences bring pain.

(c) The greater the difference between my position and the stimulus's position, the greater the absolute sensation resulting from the stimulus. So, absolute sensation is proportional to the distance to the stimulus.

(d) One's position decreases while experiencing pain and increases while experiencing pleasure. One's position increases quickly while experiencing intense pleasure and moderately while experiencing mild pleasure, and vice versa for pain. So, the rate of change in one's position is

proportional to the distance to the stimulus.
(e) By (c) and (d), absolute sensation is proportional to the rate of change—also known as the first derivative—of one's relative position.
(f) A mathematical model can be formulated from these observations. The resulting absolute sensation from a given stimulus function can be derived by solving a first-order differential equation.
(g) By knowing what kinds of absolute sensation functions cannot occur, one can derive which corresponding stimulus functions cannot exist.

Altruism

Humans are an interesting lot. We are the only species that has been observed to give money, time, and energy unselfishly to causes that we feel *ethically* committed to. No other species acts unselfishly.

What about the dog that cares for her pups until they are strong enough to find food and shelter on their own? Is this unselfish behavior? Not in an evolutionary sense. The dog attempts selfishly[4] to protect its species and to flourish; if it did not care for its young, it would fail in this mission.

Let's say that an altruistic dog did exist. Instead of raising its own children, it simply looked for sick birds

---

[4]I use the word *selfishly* with a certain reservation. The dog probably does not consciously choose to guard its existence and its offspring, or to protect the canine species. But it does follow the instinctual instructions that were encoded by its *selfish genes*.

and nursed them back to health. There are two mutually exclusive possibilities for the source of its altruistic behavior: either it's genetic or it isn't. If it isn't, then there is no guarantee that the same behavior would be passed on to any offspring. If it *is* genetic, then the gene has no chance for survival because the dog refuses to reproduce, its time being spent helping birds with broken legs. Well, can't a dog be altruistic and still reproduce? Let's see.

The animal world, far detached from the human world, is a constant struggle for survival. In a colony of any given species, only a fraction of the beings will be able to reproduce, the rest of them being sterile or eaten or killed by nature before adolescence. Of those who are able, only a fraction will successfully reproduce, due to competitive selection by the female and the ability of the female to bear her children before being killed or eaten. Of those born, only a fraction will be fast enough, smart enough, or strong enough to survive to adolescence, and the cycle begins again. Okay, so the animal world is very competitive. Does this still preclude altruism?

What about a strong, quick species that was naturally selected to survive, yet accidentally[5] acquired a genetic trait for altruism? Because the species is selected to survive with little effort (which is already highly unlikely), it has extra time to help a beaver build its bridge or a squirrel gather its nuts. Unfortunately, by the very nature of natural selection, the competition for survival becomes more stringent each and every day.

[5]Keep in mind that *everything* is nature is accidental. The evolution of sand to intelligent living creatures was an accident of galactic proportions.

After numerous generations, what used to be *child's play* to this particular species first becomes *competitive* and eventually becomes an all-out *struggle*. The altruistic members of this species will no longer be able to support others, much less themselves, and the only survivors (and reproducers) are those that act selfishly for themselves and their species. Altruism is not and cannot be found in wild nature.

How are humans any different? Today, a single person can power a machine that is capable, for example, of producing the food for ten thousand people. Since food is the only real consumable that requires effort—water can be drunk from natural springs or rivers—what do those other 9,999 people do?

Some of them build comfortable shelters, far more advanced than any shelter found in nature. Some of them manufacture clothing, even when clothing isn't needed, like in warm environments. Some of them design transportational vehicles, even though you don't really have to *go* anywhere to survive. After all, if your parents survived where you are, and so did your grandparents, then why can't you? When all the mansions and Ferraris and space shuttles and chocolate-covered grasshoppers are said and done, people still have limitless time to pursue their hobbies and interests[6]. Much like the evolution of life, hobbies and interests are also prey to

---

[6]The Unabomber in his *Manifesto* refers to activities which are not necessary for survival or reproduction as *surrogate activities*. By this definition, the only difference between our activities and those of wild animals is that most of ours are surrogate.

evolution, but a much quicker kind, called *cultural evolution*. One interest that has evolved and survived for many years, for one reason or another, is altruism.

What is altruism? It is a state of mind in which one attempts to increase another's pleasure or decrease another's pain. It is *not* altruistic to give money or time to one's children; here, the continuation and success of one's lineage is at heart. Investments are *not* altruistic. To provide education and scholarships to our community's youth is an *investment* with hopes that the youth will continue where the previous generation left off. For example, I receive many engineering scholarships whose purpose is to increase the number of competent engineers in America. Such investments do, in fact, serve their purpose, and do not demonstrate the same detrimental effects that altruism does.

Many people live comfortably, which means that they can support themselves with minimal effort and have few worries about their own survival. They have time to pursue their hobbies and interests, which means that they have time to pursue pleasure. Those that have acquired an interest in altruism often want to *even things out* a little: to narrow the gap between the *haves* and the *have-nots*. They want to give. For what purpose? Is it to give others pleasure—i.e. to make others happy? To reduce their pain? If so, does altruism serve its purpose?

As we've seen in this chapter, a person is at a certain position at a given time. Depending on the stimuli she is perceiving, this position may be changing. By stimulating her positively, her position will increase and she will experience pleasure until she becomes used to the stimulus. Conversely, the purpose of *revenge* is to stimulate a person negatively and thereby inflict pain. So, even if a millionaire is at a higher relative position than is the ghetto boy, neither one of them will experience pleasure or pain unless acted upon by a stimulus that differs from their present position.

It is no wonder, then, why money doesn't bring happiness. Making money can be pleasurable, because it can result in a constant increase in position. But once that stimulus is gone, the millionaire will experience no more pleasure due to his money. I don't care how rich he is. In fact, making money does not necessarily have to be perceived as a positive stimulus. It is believable that a millionaire might envy the freedom of a vagrant, or the carelessness of a sidewalk juggler, or the laughter of a poor father and his loving family. In that regard, losing all of his money might be pleasurable.

So I've got two questions. First, who's to say that the poor boy in the ghetto is at any lower of a position than the arrogant altruist who tries to "help" him? Second, even if the ghetto boy *is* at a lower position, why is he more deserving of pleasure than anyone else? Remember—all that matters to a person at any given time is whether or not he is experiencing pleasure or pain. In the absence of stimuli, both the boy and the millionaire feel neither pleasure nor pain. And just as the millionaire eventually gets used to his money, which no longer brings him pleasure, the boy gets used to his poverty, which no longer brings him pain.

Now, let's *assume* that the poor boy is at a very low position relative to the rest of society, which most people would agree with. The only way for that boy to experience pleasure is to be stimulated by a higher position. But since he is lower in position than society, then it is easy for him to find a positive stimulus. Similarly, there are not many stimuli lower in position than he is. So, he is more likely at any given time to be stimulated by a higher position than a lower position; he is more likely at any given time to be feeling pleasure than pain. Yet, the millionaire with the beautiful wife, children, and the best friend money could buy doesn't have much to look forward to. His position is so high that, virtually anywhere he turns, he is stimulated by a lower position. It is much more difficult for him to find pleasure since, unfortunately, he already has everything.

So if you're going to be an altruist, help those who really need it: those who already have it all. Since the disadvantaged are usually most concerned about their own health or well-being, most altruists are those who already have everything they need, and are usually at a very high position with regard to society. It seems most conclusive to me, then, that the people who need the most help are the altruists themselves.

I do not intend to offend any altruists. I recognize their intentions and I respect and admire them. I am simply stating that the very purpose of altruism may not be served. Altruism is certainly not a friend, but a foe?

You're a Big Sister. You take your little sister to an amusement park, and then to a movie, and then you buy her a triple-scoop ice cream cone. You gave her pleasure. Your purpose is served. Right? You take her home, where she has to face her hunger, uncleanness, and abusive mother again. Now, in the absence of the pleasure she felt today, she will feel more pain than if you had never taken her out. Why? Let's analyze our mathematical model again.

When you exposed her to a higher position, she experienced pleasure because her position began to increase toward the stimulus itself. But now when she is faced with her previous (low) position, she must ultimately fall back to that position, experiencing pain in the meanwhile. Even though she perceived her mother's abuse as a negative stimulus before, she now perceives it as a more intense negative stimulus.

Another example. Your son is having a hard time paying his bills, so you help him out for a while. Eventually, he gets used to the ease with which he is getting by, and when you finally set him free, his bills are going to come as a painful slap in the face. The only way to get around this necessary evil is to continue paying his bills forever (assuming you could outlive him—or perhaps you'll kill him first). Unfortunately, your altruism will afford him pleasure only for a little while. Eventually, his position will level out, his pleasure will diminish, and your altruism will simply become a quest for pain avoidance.

So perhaps altruism can have reverse effects. If you are an altruist, you should seriously consider the effects of each individual act of your altruism. If you give a person a dollar, will that keep that person from learning how to earn that dollar himself? If you teach a person what you believe, will that close the person's mind to other possibilities? If you help a person escape from his problems, will that prevent the person from learning how to solve them? If you teach a person how to solve his problems, will that steal from him the pride of discovering the solutions himself? If you bring pleasure to one person, is it fair that you cannot simultaneously bring pleasure to someone else, who is just as worthy?

For all of these reasons, I can observe the detrimental effects of altruism everyday.

Applying the Model

Prison. Is it painful? For the whole thirty or forty years? Prisoners can read, play games, watch TV, and drink milk. Prison may not be the Hilton but I know for sure that prisoners aren't always experiencing *intense pain*. You'd think the modest pain they experience would diminish to zero within the first few months. So how do you expect an additional forty years' time to be anything but a mooch off society? Prison needs to be intensely painful without the possibility of this pain significantly diminishing. If not, how do we expect the thought of prison to deter criminals? And it doesn't, so it's time to apply these principles to the criminal justice system[7].

Welfare. We support young, poverty-stricken mothers because we hold fast to the altruistic belief that they have the right to live and reproduce. Does it bring them pleasure to be uneducated, dependent, and constantly pregnant? Are we doing them a favor by feeding and housing them? Would they be any less happy dead (or better, *struggling*)? Probably not. This altruism is senseless. Do they have the right to live? Do they have the right to reproduce? Do they have the right to burden society? Nature would say no. That's a fact. As a firm

---

[7]Some would argue that the purpose of prison is not to *correct* criminals, but to separate criminals from society.

supporter of common law, I don't condone the killing of anyone; however, keeping someone alive is a favor, not a requirement. Lots of people die every day but how often do *you* try to stop it?[8]

Chapter Conclusions

What kind of stimuli will result in eternal pleasure or eternal pain? By applying the mathematical model in this chapter, it is possible to determine what kind of a stimulus will create a known sensation. Eternal pleasure/pain can only be created by an infinitely increasing/decreasing stimulus. A constant stimulus—e.g. a backrub—will lose its sensation over time, so only a backrub whose intensity increased forever could cause eternal pleasure. Clearly, the concept of an infinitely increasing backrub is ludicrous.

Altruism—friend or foe? The goal of altruism is to provide pleasure or help to avoid pain by exposing the person to a higher[9] stimulus. These questions must be asked.
(a) How do you know you are exposing the person to a higher stimulus? The person might perceive it as lower.
(b) Is one person more worthy than another of a random act of altruism?
(c) If so, shouldn't it be the rich and prosperous who are

---

[8]Some claim that the purpose of welfare is to keep hungry people from *becoming* criminals.
[9]Higher, though not necessarily positive, such as in the case of pain avoidance.

less likely to find positive stimuli than the destitute and disadvantaged?
(d) Might the altruist ultimately be imposing just as much pain as pleasure on his victim, if not more?

Altruism does not serve its purpose and may have detrimental effects.

Exercises

Position

Problem #1: Find the position function and the absolute sensation function, where

$s(t) = p(t) + p'(t)$, $p(0) = 0$, $p'(0) = s(0)$, and

(a) $s(t) = at + a$;
(b) $s(t) = at^2 - 2a$.

Absolute Sensation

Problem #2: Is absolute sensation dependent upon time or stimulus?

Problem #3: This problem is a continuation of Problem #6 in *What is Déjà Vu?* It is asked and answered in two parts, starting with Part III. Use the previous answers for the first two parts.

Part III Question: I usually get a little annoyed whenever my concentration is broken. So, say that the pleasure/pain component of sensation (a) is -20%, where pleasure is positive and pain is negative. Responding to a sound is an evolutionary function that usually brings me neither pleasure nor pain. So, say that the pleasure/pain component of sensation (b) is 0%. Hearing my name called, depending on my mood (i.e. how I perceive the stimulus), can bring me slight pleasure, in knowing that someone is thinking about me, or that I am not forgotten. So, say that the pleasure/pain component of sensation (c) is 5%. Hearing my girlfriend's voice, particularly if I have not heard it in a long time, can bring me great pleasure. So, say that the pleasure/pain component of sensation (4) is 40%. Give the values of all four absolute sensations.

Part IV Question: How much pleasure or pain does Ernold experience at T? Graph the sensation vectors, add them together, and show that the projection of the summation vector onto the pleasure/pain axis is, in fact, how much pleasure or pain Ernold experienced at T.

Pleasure/Pain Experienced

Problem #4: Lou's absolute sensation function happens to be very predictable.

$AS(t) = \sin(t)$,

where t is measured in hours. How much pleasure or pain has Lou experienced

(a) In $\pi/2$ (about 1.6) hours?

(b) In 2π hours?

(c) As time$\rightarrow\infty$?

Problem #5: If one's position were increasing like
$\triangle p(t) = 6e^{2t}$,

where t is in units of days, then
(a) What is the resulting time-dependent (net) absolute sensation function?
(b) How much pleasure or pain has the observer experienced in the first week?
(c) How does this number compare to an orgasm, which lasts on the order of seconds?

Solutions

Answer #1:
(a) The correct solution is $p(t) = at$ and $AS(t) = a$, so absolute sensation remains constant.

(b) The correct solution is $p(t) = at^2 - 2at$ and $AS(t) = 2at - 2a = 2a(t-1)$, so absolute sensation grows linearly, with slope = 2a.

Answer #2: A sensation is *only* a function of the stimulus that caused it. The function, itself, may not always be the same; it depends on the *mood* of the observer. For example, a person might perceive an identical stimulus different ways at different times, therefore experiencing different absolute sensations as a result of that stimulus. But at any given time, there is some absolute sensation *function machine* which maps stimulus directly to absolute sensation.

Throughout this book, absolute sensation function is often written as a function of time. Is this valid? Absolute sensation is dependent on stimulus, and stimulus is dependent upon time[1], so absolute sensation is

---

[1]One perceives one set of stimuli one minute and a different set the next.

dependent upon time by

asf(st(t)) = AS(t),

where st(t) is the time-dependent stimulus, asf(st) is the stimulus-dependent absolute sensation, and AS(t) is the time-dependent absolute sensation.

Answer #3: (Answered in two parts.)

Part III Answer: AS_n = pleasure/pain component of AVS_n = $(PC_n)(AVS_n)$.
$AS_1 = (PC_1)(AVS_1) = (-20\%)(35\%) = -7\%$.
$AS_2 = (PC_2)(AVS_2) = (0\%)(14\%) = 0\%$.
$AS_3 = (PC_3)(AVS_3) = (5\%)(28\%) = 1.4\%$.
$AS_4 = (PC_4)(AVS_4) = (40\%)(63\%) = 25.2\%$.

Part IV Answer: Ernold's pleasure or pain at T is the sum of all the absolute sensations he received at T. $AS_1 + AS_2 + AS_3 + AS_4 = 19.6\%$, which is positive and therefore pleasurable.

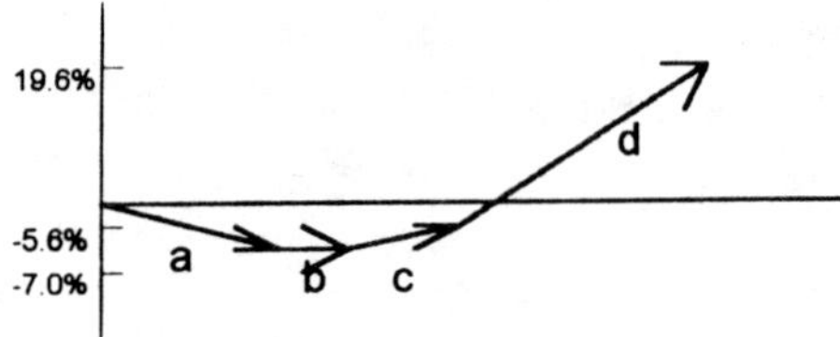

Answer #4: Pleasure/pain experienced is the definite integral of the absolute sensation function with respect to time. So,

$$\text{(a) } PE = \int_0^{\pi/2} \sin(t)dt = 1.$$

$$\text{(b) } PE = \int_0^{2\pi} \sin(t)dt = 0.$$

(c) For this function, there is no limit for the indefinite integral as $t \to \infty$; it simply keeps bouncing between -1 and 1. However, it can be said that Lou's pleasure/pain experienced as a fraction of time approaches zero, because

$$\lim_{t \to \infty} \frac{-\cos(t)}{t} = 0.$$

Answer #5:

(a) $AS(t) = \frac{dp(t)}{dt} = 12e^{2t}$.

(b) $PE = \int_0^7 12e^{2t}\,dt = 1{,}202{,}598$ days of pure pleasure.

(c) Let's say that an observer is 100% conscious as he experiences an orgasm. The orgasm, itself, monopolizes maybe 90% of his consciousness, and perhaps 80% of it is absolute pleasure. The resulting absolute sensation is (100%)(90%)(80%) = 72%. Assume that the absolute sensation remains constant throughout the orgasm, which is a fair assumption since it takes more than a few seconds for a sensation to diminish. Lastly, say that the orgasm lasts five seconds, which is about 0.000058 of one day. The pleasure experienced is, then, (72%)(0.000058) = 0.000042 (days of pure pleasure). When compared to the calculation in part (b), it's clear that the position function introduced in Problem #5 is not realistic.

Do Heaven and Hell Exist?

Do Heaven and Hell Exist?

In this chapter, we are going to apply our mathematical model to the realm of Heaven and Hell and show that these concepts are out of phase with what we observe. We'll also apply our virtual reality/still frame perspective to arrive at an answer regarding the existence of Heaven and Hell that only depends on one's existence.

Feelings

Heaven and Hell are all about pleasure and pain. It doesn't make any sense to talk about these entities without also talking about the pleasure or pain that accompany them. It doesn't seem to matter *where* they are, or what *color* they are. What matters is how a person *feels* inside them. For this reason, the mathematical model developed up until this point has been centered around the concepts of pleasure and pain, and this chapter is also primarily concerned with pleasure and pain.

In this chapter we are going to look at Heaven first as a place where one experiences pure pleasure (and vice versa for Hell). Then we are going to look at it as a place where one experiences just a little bit more pleasure than pain. Then we are going to look at it as a place where one experiences mostly pleasure, but with some pain. I have decided to present these arguments in this order, because this is the order of their difficulty. I will also provide both mathematical and logical arguments repudiating all three possibilities of Heaven (and Hell).

First, let's do a few thought experiments on pleasure and pain--i.e. feelings. Consider your own state. How do you feel right now? Are you being pleasured by reading this book, or is it somehow painful? What are you focused on right now? Are you completely focused on the book, or do you have a recurring itch on your right leg? Do you have to use the bathroom, and are you just too lazy to get up and go right now? Let your consciousness shift a little, and pay attention to the other stimuli affecting you.

How does your body feel? Is there anything that hurts? What about your tummy? Is it hungry? Does it seem reasonable that your hunger can ever provide pleasure, or is hunger simply a quest for pain avoidance? When you are hungry, is it not pleasurable to eat, or does the removal of the hunger pain simply *appear* pleasurable? Is there a difference between pleasure and the removal of pain?

What is the air temperature? Is it too hot or too cold, or is it comfortable? Can the air temperature itself bring you *pleasure*, or just the absence of pain (of cold, for example)? What about when you come inside from the cold? Can the warmth be pleasurable?

Take a break from reading and lightly touch your left forearm with your right hand. Tickle it. Experience the slight pleasure. Try to notice all components of pleasure and pain presently affecting you.

Does it seem reasonable that you can purposely experience pleasure or pain right now, depending on what you choose to focus on? If your consciousness is completely focused on the pleasure of tickling your forearm, is it possible to simultaneously experience the pain of your hunger?

Now slap your forearm. Hard. Experience the slight pain. Does it matter to you now that you experienced the pleasure of tickling it just a minute ago?

I might even be so bold as to say that it doesn't matter how you felt yesterday, an hour ago, or even a second ago. What you are perceiving, you are perceiving *now*. So we revisit the Virtual-Reality Still-Frame perspective, where all that matters is what you perceive right now.

Still-Frame Perspective Revisited

The way one feels at any given time appears independent of how he has felt at any time in the past. That doesn't mean that the past can't affect how one feels. If I think into the past about some stimulus that gave me pleasure, I can attempt to recreate that stimulus and therefore obtain some pleasure from the thought. But if I were to notice that *I am happy*, then it makes no difference how I felt yesterday, a week ago, a year ago, or even two seconds ago, because right now I am happy, for whatever reason. If I am in Hell and Satan is whipping my behind with chains, and all of a sudden he stops and a beautiful girl kisses me, then I would feel pleasure, regardless of Satan.

This is not a perfect example, because physical stimuli can continue to be painful even after the original stimuli are gone. In the above example, my behind may continue to "hurt like hell" even after the devil stops whipping it, simply because of the physical nature of my nerves. But I think you get the idea. If until now I have been experiencing only painful absolute sensations, and then all of a sudden I experience only pleasurable absolute sensations, then I am feeling pleasure—regardless of how much pain I felt previously.

This is analogous to the Still-Frame perspective presented in *Is There an Afterlife?* It is never yesterday. Tomorrow never comes. It is always now. And, *at now*, one is experiencing certain sensations which are perceived as either pleasurable or painful, irregardless of what one perceived previously.

So, even if pleasure and pain *experienced* are measurable quantities—defined in this book as the timed integral of net absolute sensation—it doesn't really make much sense to talk of how much pleasure or pain one has experienced. Sure, maybe it allows for interesting conversation. Your Navy uncle sure does like telling you about 'Nam. And your courageous 12-year-old nephew loves talking about his go-cart accident last month—and he didn't even cry! But what happened in the past does not change that they are happy or unhappy right now. What has happened in the past does not give a person any valuable information as to whether he can expect to feel pleasure or pain in the future.

Don't get me wrong. Talking about pleasure and pain isn't completely useless. If your dad tells you how it felt when his big toe got caught in a bicycle chain, then that information might keep you from doing the same thing. And it's certainly useful to avoid pain. If the body-pierced purple-haired dirtrocker down the street tells you what a kick-ass time he had playing mailbox baseball last night, then that information might be useful in determining if you, too, want to experience those same kind of stimuli. And if you are fourteen, and your boyfriend tries to tell you how pleasurable sex would be if you'd only give it a try, well, he's probably not a very reliable source.

Don't forget that people can only describe stimuli. Even in describing sensations, they can only refer to other stimuli. For example, "It felt good. I was excited. It felt like the time that my dad came home after the war." What you consider good, I may not. What excites you may not excite me. It is impossible to communicate sensations directly.

Stimuli are the international multi-language media. Playing mailbox baseball is a stimulus. Playing in the middle of the night is another stimulus. Hanging with your friends is another. And avoiding cops is yet another. These stimuli can be communicated. But even though these sensations were pleasurable to the dirtrocker down the street, they may not be pleasurable to you.

In that regard, you are in your own virtual reality, and I in mine, where we are affected by stimuli that may or may not be absolute (unchanging). If I am in pain right now, then regardless of how I felt ten minutes ago, I am still in pain right now.

How much pleasure or pain have I felt in the past? is not a useful or even valid question. Who cares? If you have lived a dirty, hungry, destitute life, the mere fact doesn't change how you feel right now. I am not interested in how I have felt in the past. I am interested in how I will feel in the future. The past is gone. I have already experienced it. Even if I try to remember those experiences, the best I can do is create new stimuli in my mind which emulate the original stimuli. But I cannot consciously relive the same sensations or experiences that I lived in the past. They're gone.

The more appropriate question is *How much pleasure or pain will I feel in the future?* The remainder of this chapter will address and attempt to answer this question.

Pleasure and Pain Uninterrupted

First we will look at the possibility of eternal, uninterrupted pleasure and pain.

What exactly does it mean to feel more pleasure than pain? Since pleasure and pain experienced were defined in *Altruism—Friend or Foe?* as the timed integral of net absolute sensation, the question must be asked with respect to time. For example, "How much pleasure or pain will I experience tonight on my date with Esmerelda? What about within the next ten minutes?

Will the coming year bring me more pleasure or pain? What about—dare I ask—eternity? In other words, will I ultimately experience more pleasure or pain?"

Let's start with the last question and work backward. It's a little bit tricky, so let's start with an even easier question that will lead us in the right direction. *Will I experience eternal pain, beginning at some point in time?* Christians claim that after a certain point in time, referred to as Judgment Day, damned souls *shall go away into everlasting punishment: but the righteous into life eternal.* [Matthew 25:46] Hell is further described as a *lake of fire* in Revelation 20:15. As a Christian for the first many years of my life—but not by my own free and clear choice—I feel justified in combining these two descriptions into one definition: Hell is a place where one experiences eternal, uninterrupted pain. Inversely, Heaven is a place where one experiences eternal, uninterrupted pleasure. Not all Christians would necessarily subscribe to these definitions, but most would.

Some Christians claim that Heaven is a place where a person is eternally "one with God," whatever the hell that means. But ultimately, Heaven doesn't mean anything at all unless this "oneness" is perceived as pleasurable. If this "oneness" is painful, then Heaven is Hell, and there is no motivation for getting into Heaven. If this "oneness" is an absence of any feeling, or at least a complete absence of pleasure and pain, then again it is not something that is desired. Ultimately, this oneness must appear at a higher position than the observer, otherwise Heaven isn't really Heaven. So if this oneness *is* at a higher position, then it would be perceived as pleasurable.

There are many other concepts of Heaven, all of

which must possess the element of pleasure, in some form or another. As noted in *What Are the Detriments of Christianity?*, the fact that so many interpretations of Biblical "truths" exist is evidence that most of them, if not all of them, must be false. So, in order to completely discredit the Christian concepts of Heaven and Hell, I must present and repudiate all possibilities, which this chapter will attempt to do.

As stated previously, I will first venture into the most popular Christian view, that Hell is a place where one experiences eternal, uninterrupted pain, and vice versa for Heaven.

Only the following two mutually exclusive possibilities exist.

(A) It is possible for me to experience eternal, uninterrupted pain beginning at some time T. Perhaps T is my death or *judgment day*.
(B) It is not possible for me to experience eternal, uninterrupted pain.

Assume (A) is the truth.

(i) It is possible for me to experience eternal, uninterrupted pain beginning at some time T.
(ii) After T, I will experience no pleasure.
(iii) At T, I will re-experience all sensations previously perceived infinitely many times in the future.
(iv) I have experienced pleasure, which is a sensation.
(v) At T, I will experience pleasure infinitely many times in the future.
(vi) Contradiction with (ii). Statement (i) is statement (A)

is false.
(vii) So, statement (B) is true. It is not possible for me to experience eternal, uninterrupted pain.

Using the above definition of Hell, I'll continue this argument.

(viii) Hell is a place where I will experience eternal, uninterrupted pain.
(ix) So, it is not possible to experience Hell.
(x) Hell does not exist.
(xi) Similarly, Heaven does not exist.

Don't let statement (iv) above confuse you. One could theoretically receive pleasurable sensations within a net painful experience. However, this does not contradict statement (iv). When one realizes that he is experiencing pleasure, that *realization*, itself, becomes a stimulus that he perceives as a sensation. This sensation may or may not be pleasurable itself, but it must be able to be recalled again. And the only way to recall that sensation is to have an identical perception: the perception that one is experiencing pleasure.

In other words, the belief (perception) that I am experiencing pleasure is a sensation that I must perceive infinitely many times. Is it possible to experience a net painful sensation while believing that I am experiencing pleasure? Of course not, because the pain itself is a perception that would preclude the belief that I am perceiving pleasure. If I believe that I am perceiving pleasure, then I am perceiving pleasure, because a perception *is* a belief (and perhaps nothing more).

It's true, an identical perception (sensation) will not necessarily come from an identical stimulus. In other words, some may argue that the person may not "actually" be experiencing pleasure (the stimulus) when he receives the sensation of pleasure; he must only *think* he is experiencing pleasure in order to experience that sensation. Again, this reservation is absurd, since pleasure is a perception—an observation—and to *think* that one is experiencing pleasure is, in fact, to perceive pleasure. If I were to hold my hand in a fire and perceive it as pleasurable, it wouldn't really matter if the stimulus *usually* results in pain; all that matters is that I perceive that stimulus as pleasurable.

(XVIII) I will never experience eternal, uninterrupted pain or pleasure.

This appears to show that Heaven and Hell don't exist. Unfortunately, in a desperate search for evidence that will uphold the bad Good Book, some Christians will want to modify their description of Hell so that the above argument does not preclude it. They'll claim that maybe, just maybe, Hell is eternal pain with occasional interruptions of pleasure. In other words, maybe Hell is a place where one experiences more pain than pleasure, and Heaven as vice versa. Let's analyze this objection.

Pleasure and Pain Surpluses

A pleasure or pain surplus is simply a positive or negative value of pleasure/pain experienced. Let's say that when you woke up this morning, your position was zero, by convention. Maybe your wife feels frisky, and you start the day with a little love. Your position is certainly positive, for you have experienced pleasure. Does that mean that you are in Heaven? If Heaven is simply a surplus of pleasure, how is Heaven any different from the day-to-day pleasures of your life?

Maybe you go into work, only to find that your company can't afford you anymore. The fear and frustration of your newfound unemployment is certainly greater in magnitude than the pleasure of sex this morning. So now your position is negative, implying that you have experienced a pain surplus. Is this Hell? If Hell is simple a surplus of pain, then how is Hell any different from the day-to-day pains of your life?

Let's consider the pleasure/pain model again. Does Heaven imply a *finite* positive stimulus? If so, then the resulting pleasure (positive absolute sensation) will eventually diminish to zero, regardless of how *high* the stimulus is. It will take longer for one's position to approach a high stimulus than a low one, but in both situations, the resulting pleasure will (eventually) approach zero. If Heaven is a constant positive stimulus, then the pleasure that one experiences will eventually fade to nothing. In other words, Heaven will get more and more dull over time. Eventually, Heaven won't be Heaven anymore. It will simply be the absence of feeling.

It's kind of like the analogy of the millionaire. The millionaire is certainly at a higher position than most of society. So, say that Heaven is simply a place where one is disgustingly rich for eternity. After a while, though, the pleasure of wealth diminishes to zero, and

Heaven stops being Heaven.

It was shown in *Altruism--Friend or Foe?* that only a infinitely increasing stimulus could produce an absolute sensation that did not approach zero. So maybe Heaven is a place where one feels an infinitely increasing stimulus *blotched* with an occasional negative stimulus. In other words, since Heaven can't be eternal, uninterrupted pleasure, then maybe there are a few occasional interruptions. Maybe Heaven is a place where one experiences *mostly* pleasure. Even simpler, perhaps Heaven is a place where one experiences more pleasure than pain—a *pleasure surplus*.

I cannot think of any other possible definition or description of Heaven. If I can disprove this possibility of Heaven, then no other possibility of Heaven remains. After all, if Heaven is not a place where one at least experiences more pleasure than pain, then how could it be any different from Hell? I believe that I *can* disprove this possibility of Heaven, both mathematically and logically. Using equations (3) and (5) from *Altruism—Friend or Foe?*, we find that the total amount of pleasure or pain one receives between T_1 and T_2 is shown by,

$$PE = p(T_2) - p(T_1). \tag{1}$$

So one has experienced pain between T_1 and T_2 if her relative position is lower at T_2 than it was at T_1; she has experienced pleasure if her relative position is higher at T_2 than it was at T_1. So what does it mean to ultimately experience more pleasure than pain, starting now? It means that by the *end of eternity*, one is at a higher position than he is right now. His $\Delta p(\infty)$ must be positive.

Finite Pleasure/Pain Surpluses

The *average* pleasure or pain experienced between T_1 and T_2 is the derivative (slope) of the line connecting the two points. If one's $\Delta p(\infty)$ is finite, then the average pleasure he receives at any time is zero. Whether or not Δp approaches a *specific constant* as time approaches infinity is irrelevant. As long as the function does not approach infinity as time approaches infinity--i.e. as long as the function remains finite--then there exists some maximum value of Δp that, when averaged over eternity, results in an average absolute sensation of zero.

Take, for example, the function $\Delta p(t) = \sin(t) + 2$. Certainly this function fails to approach any value, because it keeps oscillating between 1 and 3. In other words,

$$\lim_{t \to \infty} \Delta p(t)$$

does not exist. However, $\Delta p(t)$ has a maximum at the value of 3, so that $\Delta p(t)$ averaged over eternity is zero. This is because the average slope of p(t) from 0 to ∞ =

$$\lim_{t \to \infty} \frac{p(t) - p(0)}{t - 0} = \frac{(\text{maximum of } 3)}{\infty} = 0. \qquad (2)$$

This simply shows that the sum of all pleasure and

pain one experiences averaged through time will approach zero, if one's pleasure or pain surplus does not approach infinity--i.e. either the function approaches a finite constant, or the function does not approach a constant, but remains finite.

If I were to tell you that by the *end of eternity*, you will have experienced a finite amount more of pain than pleasure, should you be scared? Of course not. For many reasons. First, that pain surplus distributed over eternity is zero. Second, at *any* given time, you have experienced either more pain than pleasure or more pleasure than pain. It's nothing to fear. It's neither Heaven nor Hell; it's just life. Ups and downs. You know that someday you're mom and dad will die, which will inflict on you a finite amount of pain, but it's not something you should fear now. Third, you will never actually reach the *end of eternity*.

So if Heaven does not imply a finite amount of pleasure, then it must imply an infinite amount of pleasure, in the form of an infinite pleasure surplus. Similarly, Hell must imply an infinite pain surplus.

Infinite Pleasure/Pain Surpluses

An infinite pleasure surplus would require that the average pleasure received over time is positive--otherwise we run into the same problem as before, a finite pleasure surplus that results in an average absolute sensation of zero. So, the slope between $p(0)$ and $p(\infty)$ must be positive, satisfying the following equation.

$$\lim_{t \to \infty} \frac{\Delta p(t) - \Delta p(0)}{t - 0}$$

$$= \lim_{t \to \infty} \frac{\Delta p(t)}{t} > 0. \qquad (3)$$

Is such an inequality possible? Sure. On a mathematical level, try the function $\Delta p(t) = t^2 - 5$. Notice, then, that

$$\frac{\Delta p(t)}{t} = t - \frac{5}{t} \qquad (4)$$

so that

$$\lim_{t \to \infty} \frac{\Delta p(t)}{t}$$

does not exist because $\Delta p(t)/t$ approaches infinity as t approaches infinity, as shown by equation (4). If such a position function did exist, it would imply that the average pleasure (or pain) experienced over eternity was infinite, clearly impossible. This is impossible because, as finite beings, we are capable only of finite, measurable absolute sensations. How would one perceive an infinite sensation? It doesn't appear reasonable.

So, we must limit ourselves to position functions which, averaged over eternity, result in finite absolute sensations. The only such functions are linear functions[1], like $\triangle p(t) = 7t$. Notice, then that

$$\lim_{t \to \infty} \frac{7t}{t} = 7 \qquad (5)$$

exists, and is simply equal to a constant (namely 7).

Pleasure and Pain Limiters

It is interesting to note that a line must ultimately limit our position in the positive (pleasure) quadrant, and another line must limit our position in the negative (pain) quadrant. In other words, our position must always fall between two lines (the pleasure limiter and the pain limiter), as shown in the following diagram.

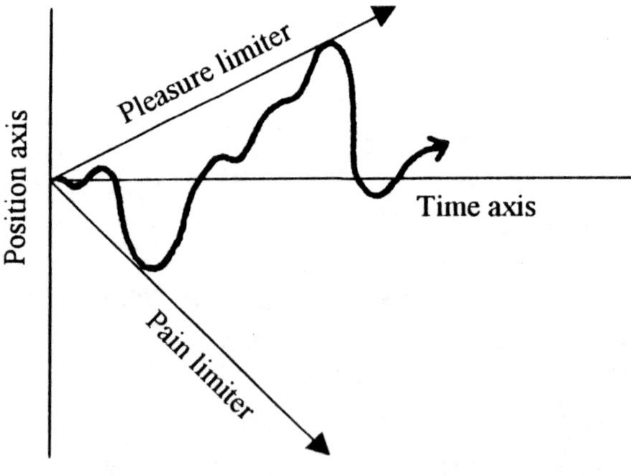

[1]This is not quite accurate, and the discrepancy will be revealed later.

This is because if our position was not bounded by linear functions, then our average absolute sensation, when averaged over eternity, would be infinite, as shown by equation (4). I'm not claiming that I know the equations for either of these lines, and I'm not even claiming that they can *ever* be known. However, there must exist pleasure and pain limiters, otherwise our experiences would not be finite.

When one's $\Delta p(T_2)$ equals one's $\Delta p(T_1)$, then one has experienced equal pleasure and pain between T_2 and T_1. So, if Heaven is to provide an average positive (pleasurable) absolute sensation, then, on average, one's position in Heaven must be increasing. That implies that one's pain limiter must be in the pleasure quadrant. In other words, there must be some line that keeps pushing one's position upward, making sure that one's position is always positive, and always increasing. We might call this the Heaven limiter, as shown in the following diagram.

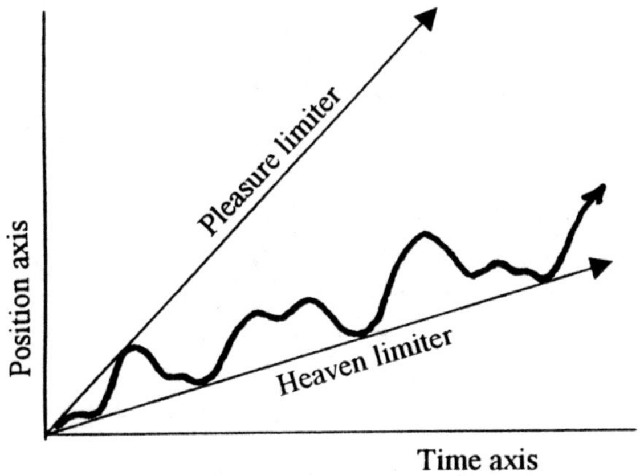

However, this line (the Heaven limiter) is uniquely different from the pain limiter explained previously. The previous pain limiter was the *result* of random, haphazard changes in one's position. It resulted from the necessity that one's experiences are finite.

To call the pleasure and pain limiting lines "limiters" is somewhat of a misnomer, in that they don't provide any force against the position function. They don't stop or push against the position function. It might be said that they can be drawn only at the end of eternity, when it is known what the position function was. All we know about the pleasure and pain limiters is that they are linear, even though we don't know their equation.

The Heaven limiter is different in that it is preset. If it weren't, then there would be no way of guaranteeing that one's position increased on the average (causing an average positive absolute sensation).

But if Heaven is to exist, and one's position were acted on by the Heaven limiter, then one's position is no longer random. Because in Heaven, it is no longer *as likely* that one experiences pleasure as pain; rather, it is *more likely* that one experiences pleasure than pain. There must be some preset line--make by God, for example--that keeps pushing one's position up... the Heaven limiter.

If there is not a linear Heaven limiter, then one's position would be finite as time approached infinity. As previously shown, this would not be Heaven, since the average absolute sensation experienced over eternity would be zero.

So, if one is in Heaven, then her position must always fall between the pleasure limiter and the Heaven limiter, both of which are lines. Likewise, if one is in Hell, then her position must always fall between the pain limiter and the Hell limiter, both of which are lines.

Say, for the sake of mathematics, that the pleasure limiter is represented by the line pl(t) = 10t and the Heaven limiter is represented by the line Hv(t) = 3t. So, one's position in Heaven must always fall between these two lines. So, the position function $\Delta p(t) = 7t$, as used in equation (5), would be possible because it falls between these two lines. This would appear to be a fair mathematical representation of Heaven, since the average absolute sensation experienced over time is positive--hence, pleasurable. Unfortunately, as shown by statement (XVIII), it is not possible to experience eternal, uninterrupted pleasure (or pain), which is exactly what $\Delta p(t) = 7t$ would provide. So, such a function is not actually possible. So Heaven cannot consist of a linearly increasing position function (which also corresponds to a linearly increasing stimulus function).

A moment ago I claimed that the only function whose average over eternity is constant and non-zero is linear. That's not exactly true. Take, for example, the position function $\Delta p(t) = \sin(t) + t/2$, which we first analyzed in *Altruism—Friend or Foe?* Notice that

$$\lim_{t \to \infty} \frac{\Delta p(t)}{t} = 0.5 \qquad (6)$$

exists, and is equal to a finite constant (namely 0.5). However, this $\Delta p(t)$ is not linear, because of the oscillating sin(t) term in it. It is important to notice, though, that the sin(t) term, when averaged over eternity, goes to zero, as shown by equation (2). Similarly, a constant, when averaged over eternity, goes to zero. There are a great many non-constant functions that, when averaged over eternity, go to zero. So, in light of these new facts, let me revise my previous statement.

The only kind of predictable[2] function whose average over eternity is constant is the sum of a linear term and other terms that average to zero over eternity. So, as an example, if $\Delta p(t) = 10t + 4 - 7\cos(t) + \exp(-3t^2)$, then

$$\lim_{t \to \infty} \frac{10t + 4 - 7\cos(t) + \exp(-3t^2)}{t} = 10 \qquad (7)$$

exists and is equal to a constant (namely 10) because the last three of the four terms average to zero as time approaches infinity.

Both such functions, utilized in equations (6) and (7), would appear to be valid functions because they both fall between two lines with positive slope. In other words, they are both limited by pleasure and Heaven limiters. But just because such functions fall between these limiters, does this mean that they represent possibilities of Heaven?

Try, for example, the previously introduced position function, $\Delta p(t) = \sin(t) + t/2$. Notice that this appears to be a completely valid position function in Heaven. It satisfies all of the following requirements.

---

[2]*Random* functions will be addressed later.

(a) It approaches infinity as t approaches infinity.
(b) Its average over eternity is a positive constant (namely 0.5).
(c) Its derivative ($\Delta p'(t) = \cos(x) + 0.5$) is sometimes positive, sometimes negative, because it oscillates between -0.5 and 1.5. This is required since I cannot experience eternal, uninterrupted pleasure or pain. This function allows me to experience *mostly* pleasure, with blotches of pain.

So there you have it. The Christians will rejoice. Here's a position function that appears to work, without violating the previous conclusions of this book. But it doesn't. You've got to look a little further. Here's why.

Renaldo and Warm Beer

Consider. Renaldo has been sober for days. He's been standing on the side of the highway in rags, holding a cardboard sign that reads, "Homeless vet. Will work for beer. God bless." Unfortunately, nobody will offer him a beer. They only throw him silver disks and green, rectangular sheets of paper, which he angrily throws back. Finally, after abandoning the highway idea and walking the slums of Gainesville, he comes across an opened glass bottle lying behind a dumpster. Inside is about one eyedropper's-full of warm liquid, and upon sniffing it, Renaldo can smell its alcoholic content. Renaldo is disgusted, but his raging need for alcohol causes him to close his eyes and down the liquid.

Renaldo's primary sensation was one of being desperate enough to drink from a dirty bottle behind a dumpster. The absolute (pain) sensation that accompanied this sensation was modest, however, because he had already been living a life of desperation and destitution. Even though Renaldo certainly perceived the dirty booze bottle at a lower position than himself, he did not perceive as *significantly* lower than himself, considering that he had already spent the entire day begging for beer. Perhaps the absolute sensation of such a sensation was -0.3. Because Renaldo was conscious of this sensation, he must relive this sensation infinitely many times in the future.

After drinking the beer, Renaldo stumbles incoherently into the road--he has a very low alcohol tolerance at this point--and gets hit by a car. After a long, drawn-out lawsuit, Renaldo is awarded a hundred million dollars, and now drinks the finest beers, wines, and liquors. Because Renaldo perceived this advance in lifestyle as very pleasurable, his position has increased significantly since the days of begging.

But Renaldo must relive all of his experiences, including the dumpster beer experience. A relived experience must also be relived with the same absolute sensation that originally accompanied it. But tell me this. How would Renaldo now perceive drinking warm beer from a dirty bottle from behind a dumpster in the slums of Gainesville? Would it be moderately painful, or extremely painful? Would it be more or less painful than when he did it the first time? It would be far more painful--e.g. with an absolute sensation of -1.4. This is because he is at such a high position relative to his previous position, that to be stimulated by the position of the dirty beer bottle now would be far more painful than it was the first time.

Therefore, it would be impossible for Renaldo to relive the dirty beer bottle experience (with the same absolute sensation of -0.3) without being at the same position that he was when it first happened. Renaldo must experience significant pain in order to reduce himself to a position at which drinking from a dirty beer bottle would only be perceived with a -0.3 absolute sensation.

For this reason, an infinitely increasing linear position function is not possible, because it would preclude the possibility of reliving sensations experienced at a far lower position. This is clearly in violation of statement (XIV).

Just for clarification, let me provide another example. Often, we hear about women who are abused by their husbands, yet they fail to file for divorce. The women often somehow justify the actions of their husbands, with statements like, "He just had a hard day at work," or "I started talking back to him, and I shouldn't have." It would be horribly insensitive of me to claim that these women don't experience pain when they are abused, because they do. However, that pain is not significant enough to drive them away from their husbands, so it must be somewhat modest, perhaps an absolute (pain) sensation of around -0.5. She must relive this sensation, with its corresponding absolute sensation, infinitely many times in the future.

Maybe one day the abusive husband is thrown in jail, and the woman has a chance to find someone new.

She meets a respectful, decent, loving man who exposes her to a better lifestyle, lacking abuse. Her position has increased, and she has been pleasured by this increase. Unfortunately, Mr. Right dies and Mr. Wrong gets parole, so she moves back in with her former husband. Since she is still at the higher position, how will she now perceive his abuse? With the same absolute sensation of -0.5? Of course not. It will be significantly more painful to her now that she is aware of a better lifestyle.

The conclusion? A sensation can only be relived from the same position it was first perceived. This excludes the possibility of an infinitely increasing or decreasing linear position function.

Using the mathematical model developed over the last few chapters, I believe I have reasonably shown that a finite pleasure surplus at the end of eternity cannot represent Heaven, because the average absolute (pleasure) sensation experienced over time would be zero. I believe I have reasonably shown that an infinite pleasure surplus by the end of eternity is not possible, for two reasons. First, any non-linear position function[3] would result in an infinite absolute sensation when averaged over eternity, clearly impossible. Second, a linear position function does not allow for the ability to relive certain past sensations, a violation of statement (XIV).

There is no feasible mathematical function that could represent Heaven or Hell.

---

[3]Or any function that is not bounded by a line, as explained previously

Heaven and Hell Limiters

What about a nonpredictable, random function that is only bound by the pleasure limiter and Heaven limiter? In other words, what if one's position were fluctuating randomly, as one's position usually does in life, when all of a sudden it hits the Heaven limiter, which pushes the position function upward, nonrandomly?

The only way such a function could occur is if there were some external power monitoring one's head, making sure that his position is always increasing on average. Whenever one's position hit the Heaven limiter, that external power would have to remove the person's free will and *force* the person to experience pleasure. Even if such a function were possible, it would steal from that person his free will, including the will to experience pain if he so desired.

Again, such a random function, bound by the Heaven limiter, is not possible, for the same reason as explained above. It would prevent a person from reliving past sensations that were experienced at a much lower position. This is also true, of course, of the concept of a Hell limiter.

Statistical Pleasure and Pain

Is there any interrelationship among past and future sensations? Yes. There must be. Because I have experienced pain in the past, I must experience pain in the future. Such a statement definitely implies an interrelationship. But how strong is this relationship?

It was shown with previous examples that, in order to relive sensations, one must be at the same position at which he first experienced those sensations. This would imply that one will be at all the positions he has ever been at before. So, whatever my position is at T_1--call it $\triangle p(T_1)$--there exists some T_2 in the future such that $\triangle p(T_2) = \triangle p(T_1)$. So, the total amount of pleasure experienced between T_1 and T_2 is equal to the total amount of pain experienced between T_1 and T_2.

This would appear to show that all experiences are interrelated, in the sense that for every bit of pleasure I experience, I will someday experience an equal amount of pain. This gives rise to the concept of *pleasure and pain debts*, which will be discussed in a moment. It would appear that if one has been suffering, then he can look forward to changing luck, a period of happiness that will follow the pain. Is this true? No, because he can't look *forward* to it; he has no idea when his position will start to increase again. It could be tomorrow; but, then again, it could be in a million years.

From an external viewpoint, it seems just as likely that I am experiencing pleasure as that I am experiencing pain. If your entire life was on videotape[4], and you randomly chose days in your past to analyze, it seems just as likely that you are laughing or singing or dancing as it is that you are crying or screaming or suffering from stomach cramps.

If you were then to plot your pleasure and pain (hence, your resulting position) on a graph with respect to time, your position would appear randomly fluctuating. It

---

[4]For example, *The Truman Show*

would have ups, downs, peaks, and troughs. There would be no predictable pattern. It would look just like the stock market on a microscopic level. The main difference, of course, is that the stock market gradually rises; one's life seems to shuffle randomly without any clear up or down trends.

So even though one is guaranteed to relive all of his sensations, and to again revisit all of the positions he has ever been at, he can't predict *when* these occurrences will happen. So, although there is an interdependence of experiences (sensations) over the long run, experiences appear random (independent) over the short run. For this reason, we will treat pleasure and pain statistically from now on.

Since the pleasure or pain you are presently experiencing appears independent of past pleasure or pain experienced, then, statistically speaking, it is just as likely that you will feel pain ten minutes from now as it is that you will feel pleasure. If you toss heads ten thousand times consecutively, what are the odds of tossing a tail the next time? Exactly one-half, assuming that the coin does, in fact, have a tail. So if you are experiencing pleasure at one moment, there is no force which is working to make you experience pain the next. There is no Heaven limiter and no Hell limiter. The pleasure and pain limiters are the result of one's change in position, so they limit one's position, per se. For these reasons, there are no *pleasure debts* or *pain debts*.

Pleasure and Pain Debts

Keep in mind that although absolute sensations

experienced from moment to moment appear independent of each other, they sometimes appear to be dependent. If, for example, you discovered your woman in bed with another man, you would probably experience pain in the form of rage or resentment. But the only possible way to continue experiencing that pain is to continue thinking about the stimuli which caused the pain: your lying, cheating, no-good woman. The least intelligent people are often observed to be the most *content*, because they more quickly *let go of* (forget) negative stimuli. Likewise, the deepest and most thoughtful people are often found to be the most distrustful and resentful of the world, because they keep reliving negative stimuli that they cannot forget. But since absolute sensations are dependent only on the stimuli that cause them, each absolute sensation is independent of every other.

I used to believe that somehow all the pleasure and pain I received canceled themselves out. It was simply an observation: some of the worst times in my life (almost always the result of a girl) were immediately followed by some of the best times in my life, and vice versa. In times of depression, I often successfully convinced myself that every passing moment of despair would someday be compensated with a moment of contentment, equal in magnitude. I believed that each stroke of good luck would be matched with an equal stroke of the bad. Whenever I realized that things were going well for me, I immediately began to worry about when my luck would end.

You might be saying that through each trial, you've always found the light at the end of the tunnel. But this *light*, was it actually *pleasure* or simply the *absence of pain*? Or maybe it was simply a reduction in pain, which one might experience as pleasure. And this brings us to another mathematical question—one that, surprisingly, will not be addressed in this book: what is the first derivative of absolute sensation? How does one perceive a change in the amount of pleasure or pain he experiences?

We only come into disagreement if that *light* was actually pleasurable. How can that be explained? When a person *despairs*, to use Kierkegaard's tongue, he often despairs over things that may not have bothered him before. When a girl is dumped by her boyfriend, she tells her friends, "My parking space is out in BFE, my classes are boring, I've been getting really small tips at work, and now my boyfriend breaks up with me to top it all off! Why can't anything go my way?" But, a week later, she's walking on air with her new stud, Jerome. Now she pays attention in her classes, only to find them interesting, she smiles at work, only to get more tips, and she even jogs to and from her parking space, just to stay slim and trim for Jerome. Is she responding to a pleasure debt? No. In her time of despair, she simply experienced pain from otherwise non-painful stimuli; when the despair disappeared, she perceived these stimuli as better than she perceived them before: a net positive absolute sensation.

So if you cry over spilled milk that was never actually spilled, then you can expect to be *relieved* (a form of pleasure) to discover the truth. And if you're positive you've got the winning lottery numbers, you can expect to be *disappointed* (a form of pain) when the correct numbers are revealed. But if you cry over spilled milk that was, in fact, spilled, there are no grounds for believing that tomorrow you'll win the lottery.

(XIX) Pleasure and pain debts don't exist.

Observing Heaven and Hell

Up until now, Heaven and Hell have been treated almost exclusively in a mathematical sense. The exception was the logical argument that repudiated the idea that Heaven could consist of eternal, uninterrupted pleasure, and vice versa for Hell.

I believe I showed reasonably well, using mathematics, that Heaven also cannot be just a surplus[5] of pleasure by the end of eternity. But I believe I can show virtually the same thing using the following logical argument, that only depends on observation.

Other than the concept of Heaven possessing the attribute of *pleasurable*, and Hell the attribute of *painful*, Heaven (and Hell) must also possess the attribute of *awareness of being in Heaven (or Hell)*. Heaven is very necessarily the result of a judgment. Either God judges you or Jesus judges you or Bill the Refrigerator Repair Man judges you--but somebody's got to. In the absence of a judgment, the composition of Heaven and Hell is chosen randomly (which is, in fact, the absence of judgment). If this were the case, then nonbelievers would have just as good a chance at getting into Heaven as Christians. And half of all the priests and ministers and bishops and popes ever living would be in Hell.

That wouldn't make much sense.

---

[5]Finite *or* infinite

And, the result of a judgment, with one's entrance into Hell must come a realization that one is in Hell. What would be the point of a punishment (or a reward) without the understanding that one is being punished (or rewarded)?

That acknowledgement can come in a variety of forms. Maybe, upon entering Hell, Satan shakes your hand and says, "Welcome to Hell." Maybe it's more subtle. Maybe nobody tells you that you are in Hell, but you realize that you are in Hell when it occurs to you that you have been roasting over a bonfire for many days. Maybe the realization is even subtler. Maybe over a period of many years it occurs to you that you have experienced considerably more pain than pleasure.

Whatever. Either way, Hell (and Heaven) must ultimately include a knowledge that you are in it. Otherwise, Hell is not a punishment that one attempts to avoid, and Heaven is not a reward that one attempts to gain.

As explained previously, I must at some point know that I am in Heaven (or Hell), otherwise Heaven does not serve the purpose of reward (and Hell the purpose of punishment).

(i) In Heaven, one experiences, on average, more pleasure than pain.
(ii) If I know I'm in Heaven, then I can always look forward to experiencing, on average, more pleasure than pain.
(iii) Contrapositive: if I can't always look forward to experiencing, on average, more pleasure than pain, then I don't know that I'm in Heaven.

(iv) Assume: I will know I'm in Heaven at time T_2 in the future.
(v) I have felt *gloomy* about the future at some time T_1 in the past. In other words, I believed that I would experience, on average, more pain than pleasure in the future.
(vi) At T_2, I must at some point in the future be able to recall the sensations I experienced at T_1. So I must at some point in the future feel gloomy about the future. By statement (iii), I won't know that I'm in Heaven at T_2. Contradiction with (iv).
(vii) Since T_2 was chosen arbitrarily, then at no time will I know that I am in Heaven. Similarly, at no time will I know that I am in Hell. Rephrased: I will never observe Heaven or Hell.

Of course, from the Virtual-Reality Still-Frame perspective, if I never observe Heaven or Hell, then these concepts are meaningless. Let me continue the argument.

(viii) Heaven and Hell are different than life as I know it.
(ix) If I observe this difference, then I will know that I am in Heaven or Hell.
(x) Contrapositive: if I do not know that I am in Heaven or Hell, then I will not observe this difference.
(xi) By (vii), I will not observe this difference. Rephrased: I will never observe a state of being that is different than life as I know it[6].

---

[6]I will never observe a state of *pleasure* and *pain* that is different than life as I know it. Whether I become a toad

(XX) I will never observe a state of being that is different than life as I know it.

One objection to this argument might be that, in Heaven, one occasionally forgets that he is in Heaven. My only response: how is that any different from life? The guts of the argument consist of the belief that one is going to experience pleasure in the future. But in life, one often feels very optimistic about the future, and then other times feels very pessimistic about the future. The only conceivable difference between Heaven and life, then, is that in Heaven one always feels optimistic about the future. This is clearly not the case. So, if there is a Heaven, it wouldn't be perceived any differently than life, with regard to pleasure and pain.

Okay, okay. So maybe Heaven and Hell exist, but I'll just never know it. That's the same as saying that I married Robyn Lively (the heartthrob of my adolescence) but she just doesn't know it yet. It's similar to the riddle, "If a tree falls and no one is around to hear it, did it make a sound?" As for me, I will never experience eternal, uninterrupted pleasure or pain; neither will I ever observe a state of being that is different than life as I know it. In other words, Heaven and Hell don't exist for me, and they will never exist to me. Whether or not there actually exists some fluffy cloud or fiery pit where unconscious, unthinking slugs go to makes no difference to me. I will never go to *Heaven* or *Hell*. Heaven and Hell don't exist.

---

or a bodiless spirit after I die is subject to debate.

(XXI) Heaven and Hell do not exist.

Fire and Brimstone

So where's the fire and brimstone now? What's to scare us believers and nonbelievers into accepting the Bible's fairy tales now? Nothing. There is no lake of fire. There is no eternal punishment. What's to tempt us to deliver ourselves from temptation now? Nothing. There is no all-encompassing kingdom of love. And eternal life is already a gift that can never be taken away. There is only life. Even my afterlife will remind me of life as I now know it, with regard to pleasure and pain.

And I'm glad, too. Heaven has certainly never been made out to be the kingdom of *pleasure*. Hell! Some of the most pleasurable experiences I've ever had are sinful, evil, shameful, wrong, immoral, unethical, wicked, and lots of other scary adjectives that I haven't thought of yet.

Heaven and Hell are inventions. They are concepts that have been imposed on the world by people who stand to benefit from this proliferation *or* by people who are infected with these harmful memes. But these concepts out of phase with what we observe.

Christianity firmly relies on the existence of Heaven and Hell. The implications of their nonexistence are disastrous to the Christian establishment.

(a) There is no incentive to living a Christian lifestyle.
(b) There is no punishment for neglecting to live a Christian lifestyle.
(c) The Bible is incorrect at least once; much like an

inaccurate history book, there is no reason to believe the Bible on accounts where the it is the only known source. Since the Bible provides no new, credible information, it serves no useful purpose.

(d) Jesus of Nazareth did not come from Heaven. If you *accept Jesus Christ as your savior*, you will not go to Heaven. There is no reason to believe that Jesus is a *messiah*.

(e) If you commit "sins," you will not go to Hell. Since sinners go to Hell[7], there is no reason to believe that anyone can sin.

(f) Need I go on?

The Pope is not a *holy* man. There is nothing particularly significant about the Pope, except that he has secured mind control over millions of devout Catholics. Either he's the most ignorant person alive, or else the most deceitful. Maybe both. No matter how chaste we believe he is, he's not going to Heaven. No matter how much he blesses you, neither are you. The titles *reverend, rabbi, clergyman, minister, priest, preacher, pastor*, and *father* and *mother* when used in a religious context, have no meaning. They are a childish attempt to establish a hierarchy of command among people who are not willing to join a military. But these religious "leaders" can only give orders to those who submit—those who believe they

---

[7]I realize that a sinner who *accepts Jesus as his savior* is fabled to go to Heaven after *judgment day*. There is no reason to get picky about the details. Ultimately, without Heaven and Hell, there is no Christianity.

will go to Hell if they don't obey their priest. I have as much business calling myself Reverend Knight—or, dare I say, Pope Andrew Frederick I—as anyone else. The word *religion*, itself, has no more meaning than the word *hieroglyphics*; both serve the vocabulary of the humanities.

Forgive my biting rhetoric. Christianity is just not a nuisance. It is not simply a disproved theory. It is a dangerous, intoxicating drug which serves to inhibit constructive questioning, natural curiosity, and intellectual thought. The idea that devout Christians would preclude the possibility of evolution from a sixth-grader's course of study only goes to show what kind of ignoramuses they are[8].

Chapter Conclusions

Do Heaven and Hell exist? No. Regardless of how one defines these words, I will never experience Heaven or Hell.

Will the future bring more pleasure or pain? The future will bring exactly what it responds to. If you subject yourself to pleasurable stimuli, you will feel pleasure. If you subject yourself to painful stimuli, you will feel pain. The amount of pleasure or pain you have already experienced has no direct bearing on how much

---

[8]Yes, I am well aware of the irony that I, myself, would preclude the possibility of Christian creationism from a sixth-grader's course of study, so don't bother mentioning it.

pleasure or pain you are feeling or will feel. There are no pleasure or pain debts. If you want pleasure, you must seek it. If you want to avoid pain, you must actively do so.

Exercises

Independence of Absolute Sensations

Problem #1: Absolute sensations are only functions of the stimuli that caused them, so they are, strictly speaking, independent of each other. Give examples of absolute sensations that *appear* to affect future absolute sensations—i.e. pains that cause pain and pleasures that cause pleasure. Then, give examples of absolute sensations that are completely independent of future absolute sensations—i.e. pleasures and pains that, once gone, are inconsequential.

Position Function Limitations

Problem #2: A position function is bound by the condition that its first derivative (absolute sensation function) must sometimes be positive and sometimes be negative. Neglecting this condition, name at least two functions $\triangle p(t)$ such that

$$\lim_{t \to \infty} \frac{\triangle p(t)}{t} > 0.$$

This limit represents the average slope of $\Delta p(t)$—the average absolute sensation—over infinity.

Pleasure and Pain Debts

Problem #3:
(a) Beatrice[1] is a moron. He doesn't think about anything. Up until now, he's been kicked around all his life. What is the likelihood that he is now experiencing pleasure?
(b) Albert is very thoughtful. In retrospect, his life has been *relatively* pleasurable. What is the likelihood that he is now experiencing pleasure?

---

[1]"Wait, Butthead—heh, heh—my name's not..."
"Shut up, Beatrice." —*Beavis and Butthead*

Solutions

Answer #1: Answers will vary, of course. However, in answering the first question, consider the stimulus of discovering that your spouse has cheated on you. This could result in a painful or pleasurable absolute sensation.

Painful: You have always trusted your spouse, and built a life with him/her. The infidelity is perceived as extremely painful. For a long time after the discovery, thinking about the pain results in more pain—so it appears as if later absolute sensations depend on the first.

Pleasurable: You have been wanting to divorce your spouse for a long time, but have found insufficient grounds for doing so. The discovery is perceived as pleasurable, for it allows you to step forward in your plans. Every time you think of the pain thereafter, you are blessed with a sigh of relief—so it appears as if the first absolute sensation affected later absolute sensations.

In both cases, however, it is only the perception of the remembered stimulus that results in the pleasure or pain.

In answering the second question, consider biting your tongue. You would probably perceive this as sharply painful, but once the stimulus is gone, the sensation is completely inconsequential. No matter how hard you think about the sensation after the pain has dissipated, you cannot feel any more pain. Whether you bit your tongue once or a hundred times today makes no difference to you now.

Answer #2: Lots of functions will satisfy this limit. The simplest is a line, such as $\Delta p(t) = mt + b$, where m and b are real numbers. Here, the limit converges to m, which means that the average absolute sensation over infinity is m. Any polynomial of degree>1 will also work, but here the limit will not converge; the limit will approach infinity as $t \to \infty$. This would imply that the average absolute sensation experienced would be infinite, which is certainly impossible in real life. An exponentially increasing function, like $\Delta p(t) = e^{t}$ would have essentially the same result, since the average absolute sensation experienced would approach infinity as $t \to \infty$. An exponentially *decaying* function, however, like $\Delta p(t) = e^{-t}$, is essentially the same sort of function we derived for a constant stimulus. The limit ultimately approaches zero, so it does not satisfy the requirements of Problem #2.

Answer #3:

(a) Since it is clear that Beatrice's brain isn't inventing any stimuli, he will only respond to external stimuli. At any given time, it is just as likely that he will experience pleasure or pain, due to the independence of consecutive sensations. So, 50%.

(b) Albert doesn't respond *only* to external stimuli, so the answer isn't as clear cut. If he is a basically optimistic person, and can attain pleasure from thinking about past experiences, then it is more likely that he is experiencing pleasure at any given time (>50%). However, if he is always missing the *good ol' days* and wishing that things could be like they used to be, then it is less likely that he is experiencing pleasure at any given time (<50%).

Is There an End to Eternity?

In this chapter, we will utilize our mathematical model and Virtual Reality/Still Frame perspective to analyze how one's perception of reality changes over time. We will use this analysis in answering the question, Is there an end to eternity?

In *What is Déjà Vu?* it was stated that one's afterlife will last eternity, which was later stated to be equivalent to, "It will not end." By definition, eternity has no end. So it would seemingly be correct to state that one will not observe an end to his consciousness. The question posed by this chapter is whether or not all memories ultimately, "by the end of eternity," converge to absolute forms. If yes, then it is as if we are now receiving information from the "end of eternity," even though we will never reach that end.

Memory Modifications

Hannibal kisses his girlfriend, Martha, and it makes him feel like a schoolboy again, all tingly inside. He knows he is experiencing intense pleasure—say, for example, an absolute sensation of 75%. The next day, Hannibal discovers Martha in bed with her old high school boyfriend, Wes. He thinks back to the day before and says to himself, "That kiss wasn't as great as I first thought it was. In fact, it was even a little bit painful the way she bit my lip."

No, wait. I misjudged Hannibal. Instead, he pities himself and thinks, "That kiss was the best feeling I've ever had. And now it's all gone. I'll never love like I loved then." And then the violins play.

In either case, Hannibal consciously *modifies* his memory. Today he believes that the absolute sensation he received from that kiss was either more or less than what it actually was, 75%.

The goal of many motivational speakers, psychologists, and hypnotists is to alter a person's perception of something in order to achieve some result. Rush Limbaugh might, for example, want to see a hypnotist about his dangerous and disgusting obesity problem. The hypnotist may be able to induce in him an involuntary aversion to Twinkies, cupcakes, Spam, and midnight grocery runs, or may induce in him a positive association with physical exercising, or both.

Anthony Ziglar is the latest fly-by-night get-rich-quick overnight success in motivational speaking. He claims that every person who is in a rut has some memory which is holding that person back. Perhaps a memory of failure, a recent death in the family, a divorce, or any number of stressful events. He tells each of his followers to think about all the good things that resulted from that event, and to think of them often. Eventually, he claims, the event will become a positive memory that not only ends the rut, but perhaps becomes an inspiration.

New example. Percy's wife left him last year and took the kids, got the house, and had sex with an alter boy in the church bathroom right in the middle of a service. Since then, Percy has been eating dog food (the meaty canned type) and has roamed the streets in the only shirt she let him keep—no pants, but a nice shirt. Recently, Percy read Mr. Ziglar's book and now looks back on his divorce as an *emancipation*. He's got no leeches to support. No mortgage to pay. And now he can pursue his real hobby, drinking. Percy has found new strength, new energy, a renewed will to live. His divorce was the best thing that ever happened to him.

Is this kind of memory alteration possible? Of course. To a certain degree. And for a certain amount of time. When Percy remembers his divorce today, he breaths a sigh of relief that he no longer has to put up with the humiliation that his wife imposed on him. But how long will he remember his divorce as pleasurable? Forever? No.

(i) I was aware that I was experiencing pain at time T_1 in the past.
(ii) This awareness was a stimulus that I perceived as a sensation.

(iii) I will always again experience this identical sensation.
(iv) If this sensation does not result from a recollection of my awareness of pain at T_1, then it is not an identical sensation.
(v) So, I will always again experience the sensation of awareness of pain experienced at T_1.

Now, assume that it is possible to permanently *modify* my memory of T_1. I'll continue the above argument.

(vi) Assume: After some time $T_2 > T_1$, I will only remember experiencing pleasure at T_1.
(vii) So, after T_2, I will never again experience the sensation of awareness of pain experienced at T_1.
(viii) Contradiction with (v). So, statement (vi) is false. There exists no T_2 to make statement (vi) true.
(ix) So, I will not permanently remember T_1 differently than I actually experienced it. Since T_1 was chosen arbitrarily, I cannot permanently alter any memory.

So, can Anthony Ziglar's method of self-motivation work? Sure. Depending on the goal. If one's goal is to overcome a past setback by thinking of it in a different light, then the therapy has a chance. However, if one's goal is to completely forget a bad experience or, in Percy's case, to permanently convert a bad memory to a good one, one shouldn't hold his breath.

Part of this chapter will deal with memory

modification. But first I'll show that memory modification is possible.

(i) I have remembered a certain experience in at least two different ways[1].
(ii) At most one of those ways accurately represented the original experience.
(iii) So, at least one of those remembrances was modified.
(iv) Memory modification is possible.

So memory modification is possible, but no modification can last eternity. This is equivalent to saying that one must be able to remember experiences accurately—without modification—at the *end of eternity*. Since the end of eternity cannot be reached, this is equivalent to saying that the sum of all modifications of a memory must approach zero as time approaches infinity.

(XXII) My modification of a memory must approach zero as the time approaches infinity.

Components of Memory Modification

What is a memory modification? Well, a memory consists of consciousness at some time T. One's consciousness at T consists of the superimposition of the sensations she experienced at T, which have pleasure/pain and non-pleasure/pain components. So a memory modification occurs when one remembers one or more of

[1]See Problem #1 in the Exercises following this chapter.

these constituent sensation vectors inaccurately[2]. Let a memory modification be mathematically defined as the difference between the correct and modified sensation vectors. By resolving each modification vector into its pleasure/pain and non-pleasure/pain components, two graphs can be made: one shows the pleasure/pain modification with respect to time, and the other the non-pleasure/pain modification with respect to time. What kinds of modifications would show up on each graph?

When Percy thinks back on his divorce today, he thinks of it better than he did when it first happened. So, today, he experiences a positive modification on his pleasure/pain modification graph of that experience[3]. If tomorrow he thinks back on his divorce and finds that he is not quite so happy, he will still experience a positive modification on this graph, but it will not be as large as today. If the next day he remembers the divorce exactly as it happened and starts eating dog food again, then he will be experiencing zero modification on this graph.

Yesterday, Joe Promiscuity had the best sex of his life with Ethel. Today, he can't quite remember her name; for some reason the name *Geraldine* rings a bell. Here, a

---

[2]Since one can only intentionally remember stimuli (not the resulting sensations), then *any* attempt to remember an experience will result in a memory modification.

[3]This assumes that Percy experienced only one sensation as the result of his divorce, which is unlikely. To overcome this problem, we can work with *net sensation*, where memory modification is the difference between the correct and modified net sensation.

memory modification has clearly taken place[4]. But remembering her name isn't necessary for Joe to remember the pleasurable sex he had, so this memory modification will appear on the non-pleasure/pain modification graph.

Cause of Memory Modifications

Certainly, most memory modifications are going to have components on both graphs. What exactly causes a memory modification? A complete evaluation is not within the scope of this book, but I imagine lots of things can cause a person to remember an event or experience differently than he originally perceived it.

First, simple human error. This would account for most memory modifications with non-pleasure/pain components. What was your locker combination in seventh grade? It may seem trivial, but the fact that you were conscious (if, in fact, you *were* conscious) when you first learned the combination requires that you are someday capable of remembering it again.

Second, the way one feels, physically or emotionally. As pointed out in *Do Heaven and Hell Exist?*, a despairing person may not only perceive things

---

[4]Even the lack of a memory is a memory modification, equal and opposite in value to the original memory, since the value of the memory is now zero. Since a person must ultimately be capable of accurately remembering all of his memories, this lends credence to the claim that the sum of all modifications must ultimately approach zero as time approaches infinity.

worse than she normally would, she might also remember things differently than they originally happened, for better or worse. For example, Hilda just broke up with her physically abusive husband, Bruce. She is experiencing emotional pain and may therefore remember her beatings from Bruce with more fondness now that he is gone.

Third—well, I'm not too sure. It doesn't really matter to me why modifications occur. I am only interested in analyzing them because they *do* occur.

Statistical Limits

I will here show that the sum of all modifications of any given memory must ultimately approach zero, where zero is a statistical limit.

(i) At any given time $T_2 > T_1$, there is nothing to preclude the possibility of an x% memory modification[5] of some sensation received at T_1, where x is some real number.
(ii) The sum of all modifications of some sensation received at T_1 must approach zero as time approaches infinity.
(iii) So, zero must be a statistical, not absolute, limit.

We know that the sum of all memory modifications of some sensation must ultimately approach zero, but there is nothing to keep a person from altering a

[5]It doesn't matter here if we are referring to the pleasure/pain modification graph or the non-pleasure/pain modification graph. They have the same properties.

memory even long after the original event occurred. So the only thing that actually approaches zero (as time approaches infinity) is an outer statistical limit. Here's what I mean.

You catch your boyfriend in bed with his high school sweetie. So you go running to your best friend and, with tears in your voice, tell her the whole story. Then you tell your mom, but this time your story is somewhat different, because you remember some new facts and (maybe) forget some less important facts. So your memory of the event has been modified significantly. Then you tell your boss, and this time you add one or two facts and shuffle the story a little bit. Again, you have modified the memory of the event, but not nearly as much as before. Then, you tell the story to each person at some Friday night party, and you find that your story is virtually the same to each person. In other words, as time progresses, significant memory modifications of the original event become less and less likely. If you were to tell the story to someone in ten years and then again in forty years, the stories would probably be almost identical. Even though thirty years is a long time interval, it is doubtful—*statistically unlikely*—that your memory would experience significant modifications during that time period.

But not impossible. Getting back to Percy. Suppose that he hadn't read Anthony Ziglar's book until twenty years after his divorce. After twenty years, it is improbable that Percy would experience a significant memory modification on his own. But all of a sudden he reads the book, becomes inspired, and actually begins recreating the divorce in his head as a positive, pleasurable experience rather than what it was: painful. Here, a significant memory modification has taken place, even though the divorce has long since passed.

So what kind of a mathematical function could represent an outer statistical limit, if this limit must approach zero as time approaches infinity? Keep in mind that a statistical limit can only imply a confidence interval. In other words, let's say that you are gambling in a casino. What is the likelihood that you walk out a winner after playing only a few hands? Well, you've got a decent shot. What about after playing all night? It's very, very unlikely. What about playing nonstop for a year? Well, let's just say that you've got a better shot at being hit by a meteorite. But there is *still* a chance, regardless how small. That's what we mean by a confidence interval.

So, in devising a memory modification limitation function, we must recognize that this function only represents a confidence interval, say, of 95%. In other words, there is a 95% chance that the memory modification will be less than the maximum. Let's try to find a function that works. What about a hyperbolically decaying function?

$$mm(t) = \frac{c_0}{t}, \qquad (1)$$

where c_0 is some constant and mm(t) is the maximum possible memory modification at time t for a confidence interval of 95%. But according to equation (1), $mm(0) = \infty$, which is an outer statistical limit at $t = 0$, the exact time of the event. If the statistical range is 95%, does it make sense that there is a 5% chance that one's memory modification at t = 0 is *beyond infinity?* No. So let's try an exponentially decaying function.

$$mm(t) = c_0(e^{-t}). \qquad (2)$$

Here, mm(0) = c_0, a constant, which means that there is some *finite* outer statistical limit at t = 0. But, then again, the memory modification of an event at t = 0 (the moment the event occurs) *should* be zero, so some might argue that neither model is correct. Unfortunately, there exists no function which constantly approaches zero where mm(0) = 0.

Since a memory modification can be positive or negative, there must exist a positive and negative outer statistical limit, like

$$mm_{top}(t) = c_0(e^{-t}) \text{ and } mm_{bottom}(t) = -c_0(e^{-t}), \qquad (3)$$

where c_0 depends on the absolute value of the sensation and on the value of the outer statistical limit, which ranges from 0% to 100%, not inclusive. Say that this limit is chosen to be 95%, as in the previous example. In the following example graph[6], the horizontal axis is chosen as time, the vertical axis is chosen as net memory modification of some sensation, and the dashed line

---

[6]Again, this graph could represent both a pleasure/pain modification component as well as a non-pleasure/pain component.

represents the outer statistical limit, which we have modeled as an exponentially decaying function.

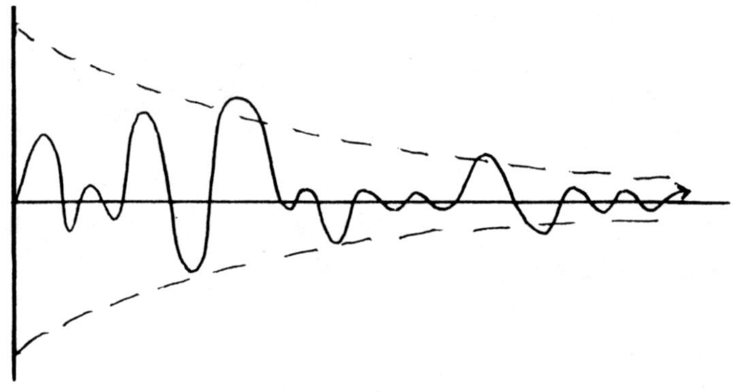

By definition, there is always a 95% chance that the net memory modification will be found between the dashed lines at any time. Since $mm_{top}(\infty) = mm_{bottom}(\infty) = 0$, net memory modification must also equal zero at $t = \infty$ by the calculus Squeeze Theorem.

End of Eternity

So the way that you perceive stimuli right now is exactly the way that you will ultimately remember perceiving those stimuli.

(i) Assume: eternity has no end.
(ii) So, there must be some point in the future T_1 after which the sum of all memory modifications remains zero.
(iii) But at some time $T_2 > T_1$, there is some finite probability that the memory could be modified.

(iv) Contradiction with (ii), so (i) is incorrect.
(v) Eternity has an end.

Time must then be thought of as a finite line segment in which one's consciousness approaches the end asymptotically. There really *is* an end to eternity, mathematically anyway. Yet one can never actually *reach* this end. So I can only experience what at the end of eternity I will remember experiencing, and in the same way. The way I feel at this moment is exactly the way I will remember feeling at the end of eternity. In that regard, one could say that it is presently the end of eternity, and I am simply reliving all of my experiences, exactly as they happened. At the very least, one could say that I am *feeling the effects of eternity*. Eternity "knows" everything that I will experience, and how I will perceive those experiences. If I can't remember an experience at the end of eternity, then I never had it in the first place. In that regard, all of my experiences are fated.

(XXIII) I am constantly feeling the effects of the end of eternity.

An Accidental Heaven and Hell

In *Do Heaven and Hell Exist?*, it was considered whether or not a person's position could displace infinitely. If so, then the average absolute sensation experienced at any given time would be positive or negative throughout eternity, not zero. Heaven and Hell were disproved in *Do Heaven and Hell Exist?* by two methods. First, that I will never experience eternal, uninterrupted pleasure or pain. And second, that I will never permanently believe that I am in Heaven or Hell. These two arguments completely preclude the existence of these entities, but there may still be those who fear the thought of *accidentally* experiencing, on average, more pain than pleasure as time approaches infinity. The independence of consecutive sensations has already been shown, so, disregarding stimuli that are invented in one's head, the likelihood of experiencing pain at any given time is the same as experiencing pleasure.

Say that every second we toss a coin; heads represents pleasure and tails represents pain[7]. Every time I toss heads, will I necessarily toss a corresponding tails? Of course not. The events are independent of each other. After a million tosses, what is the likelihood that I've tossed 500,000 heads and 500,000 tails? *Extremely small!* But how likely is it that I've tossed *between* 400,000 and 600,000 heads? Very. Let $p_h(t)$ be the percentage of heads tossed as a function of the number of tosses. So,

$$\lim_{t\to\infty} p_h(t) = 50\%. \qquad (4)$$

At $t = \infty$, there is no probability that $p_h(t) = 49\%$ or 51%. There is no probability that $p_h(\infty) = 49.999\%$ or 50.001%. There is exactly a 100% chance that $p_h(\infty) =$ 50% and only 50%.

---

[7]If it lands on its edge, then you've just won the lottery or been hit by a meteorite, which are almost equally likely.

What is the likelihood that the total pleasure you've experienced equals the total pain that you've experienced? In other words, what is the likelihood that your position today is exactly the same as it was when you first became conscious? Zero. Sure, it's possible to cross the axis between pleasure and pain, but the amount of time it took to do so is infinitesimal, which is equivalent to zero.

Here's an analogy. Let's say you want to find the exact midpoint between two points. If you run your finger between those two points, then your finger *will* at some point cross through the midpoint. But because the width of the midpoint is infinitesimal, then it took an infinitesimal amount of time for your finger to cross it.

Similarly, what is the probability at some given time that you have experienced more pleasure than pain or vice versa? 100%. It's simply life. It's nothing to fear. You can expect to always be above or below the *equilibrium* (where $\Delta p(t) = 0$). But here's the question that Christians might still be posing: *can one experience Heaven or Hell simply by chance?* Is it possible that one's position approaches infinity (or negative infinity) as $t \rightarrow \infty$? Restated, is it possible that one's average absolute sensation be positive or negative as $t \rightarrow \infty$ by pure coincidence? No.

Using the analogy above, consider the total pleasure or pain one has experienced over time as a fraction of the magnitudes of these values. In other words, over the period of one's life, he has experienced a great deal of pleasure and a great deal of pain. Say, for instance, that the magnitude of his pleasure experienced is 100,000 and the magnitude of his pain experienced is

102,000. The sum of these two is 202,000. His total pleasure/pain experienced is simply the difference of these two: 100,000 - 102,000 = -2,000, which is a net experience of pain. The fraction of this pain to the total pleasure and pain he has ever experienced is (minus) 2,000/202,000 = 0.0099, which is less than 1%. This fraction will approach zero as time approaches infinity.

For this reason, it is impossible for a person to experience an average pleasurable or painful absolute sensation due to purely random events. So, not only are Heaven and Hell impossible to perceive, the probability that a person accidentally experiences a *hellish* eternity or pleasurable eternity is zero.

So far, we've worked only with the independence of consecutive sensations. In Problems #1 and #3 in the Exercises of *Do Heaven and Hell Exist?*, it was shown that a person could relate two or more sensations—and therefore make one dependent on the other—with his mind. The stimuli invented by the mind have the same properties as external stimuli, except for the fact that they can exist by the mere will of the observer. However, any pleasure or pain that results from these stimuli will eventually diminish, since the mind is incapable of inventing an infinitely increasing or decreasing stimulus.

If I intentionally think about my girlfriend, then the probability that I will be experiencing pleasure in the next second is greater than 50%. However, from the standpoint of an external observer, it is just as likely that I am thinking about my girlfriend as it is a pap smear. In other words, lacking any further information, the pleasure or pain I feel at any given time is completely random, even though I may perceive an interdependence among some sensations.

Chapter Conclusions

Is there an end to eternity? Yes. The end of eternity is an asymptote which time constantly approaches. My consciousness is defined by the way I will ultimately (at the end of eternity) remember the individual stimuli I perceived during that consciousness. Since I am conscious, an end to eternity must exist.

Is it possible to ultimately experience an average pleasurable or painful absolute sensation? Because of the independence of absolute sensations from moment to moment as observed by an outsider, the probability of experiencing an average absolute sensation that is pleasurable or painful is zero. Even though a person's average absolute sensation is could be positive or negative for a long time, that average must eventually approach zero.

Exercises

Memory Modifications

Problem #1: In proving the existence of memory modifications, one objection to statement (i)[1] might be that, at any given time, a person is only capable of remembering a certain experience in one way. That person might believe he remembered the experience differently yesterday, but how can he be sure that he doesn't always remember past experiences exactly as they originally occurred? Respond to this objection.

Asymptote

Problem #2: If you shoot me with an arrow, the arrow will never reach me.

Let's say there are forty feet between us. Before the arrow can travel all forty feet, it must first travel twenty feet. And before the arrow can travel the remaining twenty feet, it must first travel ten feet. And before the arrow can travel the remaining ten feet, it must travel five feet, and so on. Since the distance between me

---

[1]I have remembered a certain experience in at least two different ways.

and the arrow is constantly halving, it never quite reaches me. What's wrong with this argument?

Components of Memory Modification

Problem #3: In the following plane, c represents a sensation vector as it was originally experienced and m is the modified vector in trying to remember c. Sketch the memory modification vector and resolve it into pleasure/pain and non-pleasure/pain components.

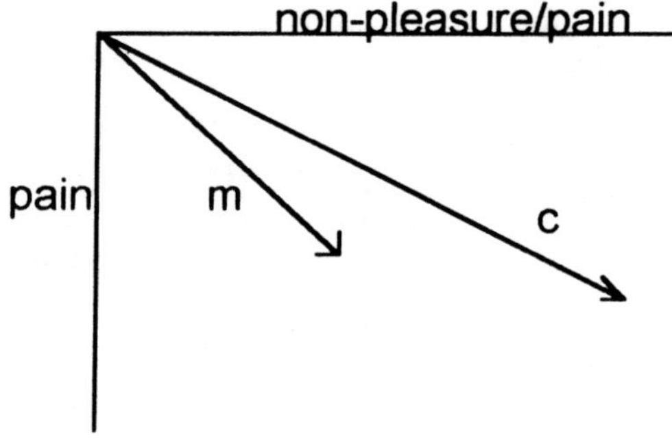

Solutions

Answer #1: All that's important is that I believe I have observed memory modifications, as in statement (iii) in the following proof.

(i) Assume: memory modifications are not possible.

(ii) At time T_2 in the past, I remembered an experience I had at time $T_1 < T_2$ in a certain way.

(iii) Today, I believe that I remember T_1 differently than I remembered it at T_2.

(iv) By (i), I remember T_1 exactly the same way I remembered it at T_2.

(v) How I believe I remembered T_1 at T_2 is different from how I actually remembered T_1 at T_2.

(vi) So, my memory of T_2 is altered or modified.

(vii) Contradiction with (i), so memory modifications are possible.

Answer #2: It only takes half as much time for the arrow to travel twenty feet as it does forty feet. And half the time to travel ten feet as twenty feet. And an infinitesimal[2] amount of time to travel an infinitesimal

---

[2]*Infinitesimal* means infinitely small or infinitely close to zero. Mathematically, *infinitesimal* is equivalent to zero.

distance. It is true that the arrow must travel an infinite number of infinitesimally short distances before it reaches me, but does that imply an infinite amount of time? No; it implies an infinite number of infinitesimally short time intervals, which is equal to some finite amount of time.

Answer #3: Here, mm is the memory modification vector.

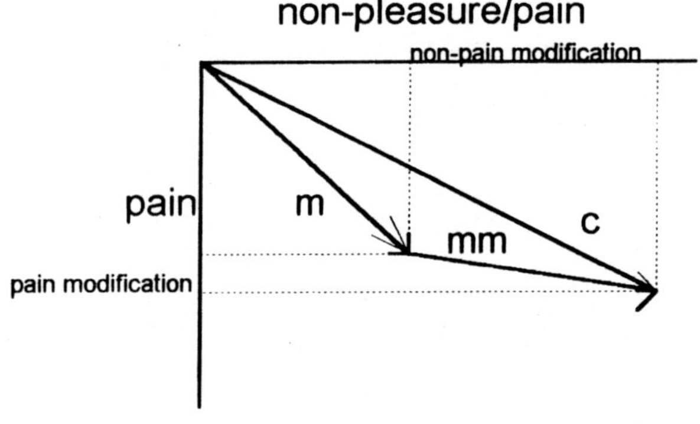

Part IV

Appendices

Afterthoughts

Afterthoughts

Thank you for reading this book. I sincerely hope that I have offered you new possibilities to ponder, a revived faith in an open mind, and a view of life, pleasure, and pain that will improve the quality of your life and your understanding of reality. There are a few additional comments I would like to present before closing.

How to Learn

A good philosopher searches for correct answers. He doesn't simply settle for the best sounding answer, or the one most in harmony with his upbringing. He must sometimes—perhaps often—suppress his former beliefs in a violent internal confrontation. The loss of security is, painful, but there is satisfaction to be found in the discovery of truth.

How exactly does one discover truth? The answer is twofold. First, stay open to all possibilities. Second, research each of those possibilities comprehensively. That's my lesson.

Maybe some things are absolutely true, while others are only apparently true. Maybe nothing is absolute. But it hardly seems reasonable to say, for example, that there may or may not be an afterlife, depending on how one looks at it. It seems like either there *is* an afterlife, or there *isn't*. It doesn't appear to depend on the observer at all. If, when my body dies, I remain conscious, then there is an afterlife. Inversely, if, when I die, I lose consciousness and never again regain it, then there is not an afterlife. It's that simple. It doesn't seem to depend on faith, or belief, or my perception of anything. It seems very black-and-white. Either there is or there isn't.

Too often people shrug their shoulders in defeat. "Andrew, you just can't prove anything. It's all a matter of faith. If you believe there's a god, great. If not, oh well. But you'll never know." Unfortunately, it seems like there *is* an answer, a correct answer, to this question, and to *any* question. I find it honorable to at least attempt to find those answers.

Certainly *searching* for answers is different than *deciding* on answers. If you want to know what is inside a locked box, then I suppose the pain of your curiosity might force you to decide what is in the box, without any evidence. You might decide to believe that there is a nuclear weapon inside. But that wouldn't be a very fun or useful belief. So you might decide that there is only air inside--again, a pretty dull belief. So, instead, you decide that there is a winning lottery ticket inside. Now *that* sounds good. You then convince yourself that in twenty years, the Box God will open the box and give you the winning lottery ticket[1].

Clearly you can see the problems involved in deciding on answers. Even if your decision was based on some evidence, your decision may be very premature. Say, for example, that the box is very dense and very heavy. You might come to the hopeful conclusion that the box is filled with gold bars, when in fact it is full of poisonous mercury.

So, in searching for answers, the first rule of thumb is not to decide on *any* answers. The moment one decides on an answer, he rules out any other possibility, regardless of the quality of evidence supporting it. This rule led me to introduce the Virtual-Reality Still-Frame perspective, an extremely conservative view that only accepts as fact that one *observes*, but not necessarily that any of her observations are accurate. The second rule of thumb is to search for evidence in the answering of a question with an unbiased, open mind. In answering questions regarding Heaven and Hell, I might, for example, answer, "I don't think that Heaven or Hell exist, but I'm open to new evidence on the contrary," or "I don't believe in Heaven or Hell for the following reasons..."

---

[1]How closely does this resemble Christianity and other religions?

Absolute Standards of Morality

Unfortunately, when people decide on answers based on insufficient evidence or no evidence at all, they become prejudice and judgmental. I might even be so bold as to state that I know very little, if anything at all. The same goes for you, most likely. Do you judge your neighbor based on her view of abortion? Do you damn your co-worker because he smokes dope? Do you verbally abuse your niece because she dances at an adult club?

Are there actions or thoughts that are *incorrect*, regardless of how they are perceived? Socrates would argue in the positive. If not, then are some actions at least *equivalent* to others? This kind of question is almost as valid as the existence of absolute standards of morality.

People Buying People

Consider. Most men would cringe at the thought of their wives or daughters stripping at an adult club or posing nude for a magazine, yet most men have visited such a club or "read" such a magazine at least once in their lives. Even some "respectable" men almost exclusively rely on such activities for sexual arousal. Is it okay for men to look but not okay for women to show? Similarly, is it okay for men to *score* but not okay for women to *put out?* In my opinion, no. I am not saying that either action is somehow immoral or absolutely incorrect, but rather that they are equivalent. I am simply claiming, without proof, that if you are a man who utilizes adult entertainment for sexual arousal, then you may want to reconsider whether or not it is okay for your wife or daughter to strip in a nude club, where profits are extremely high. And if you are a woman who sells her body for touching *or* looking, then you may want to reconsider your frustration with your husband for looking at girlie magazines.

Where is the line? If it exists, it's fine, and it can be found smack in the middle of a sea of gray. Some waitresses make more in tips than others. Is it because some are slower than others, or are incapable of bringing food to one's table? Probably not. The waitress who makes the most is the one who has the brightest smile, the one who is most attractive (physically or in character), the one who *sells herself* best. In how many ways does this differ from prostitution? I can only think of one. But the similarities are endless. Both the prostitute and the waitress rely on God-given attributes to make their money.

Consider your own occupation. Sales, politics, the media, management, you name it. They're all the same. Here's the point: *people purchase people* in the form of desirable attributes.

So how can there be any truth in a sea of gray? I don't preclude the possibility that absolute morality might exist, but I have a reasonable suspicion to believe that they don't. This suspicion might someday lead me in the right direction to devising an appropriate argument.

Abortion—the Answer is Obvious

The funny thing about any philosophy is that you

can't convince everyone. Even if you could, it's still open for debate. Just like anyone else, I get annoyed when people don't agree with me. Take, for example, the never-ending abortion issue.

> It's so obvious. When you have an abortion, you end a life. It's that simple. That baby has a right to live, just like any other human.

> It's so obvious. If you don't have an abortion, then that child is going to live a destitute, unloved, unforgiving life. It's that simple. Is ending an undeveloped life any worse than squashing a bug or eating a defenseless chicken?

Exactly. Nothing's obvious. You have to think hard and clear, absent of your upbringing, your influences, even your own views, to come across the correct answer to a question. Is there really a right answer in the abortion issue? Before you can possibly answer that question—or a slew of others—you need to learn whether or not enduring standards of morality exist. Socrates would say they do, but the Skeptics doubted him: if the world is in constant flux, then there are no enduring standards of morality.

Stealing

Is stealing *unethical?* Most people wouldn't even think about the question before responding. I certainly support common law as a general lifestyle: don't infringe on the rights of others, including the right to property. I would agree that stealing isn't very nice. I usually don't like people who steal from me. It makes me mad. It makes me want to retaliate. But is the act itself *unethical?*

Do you own a computer? Where did it come from? The store? Ultimately, it came from the earth. Yet no one asked the earth if we could have those raw materials. We *took* them. Who owns the earth? Call the maker of the earth *God*, whether or not this God is conscious; he is certainly the owner of the earth. What if God were to pick up your computer and bury it in a deep hole in your back yard? Is *that* unethical? Let's suppose for a moment that God would actually have a use for a Pentium processor. What if he just swiped it off your desk for his own personal use? Is *that* unethical? If not, then I guess it's okay for someone to steal back what has been stolen from him.

Do you own land? From whom did you buy it? From whom did the seller buy it? Go back in history and you'll find that the first owner never bought it; he *claimed* it. But how did that person know that the land was not already claimed, or did he steal it from someone else—e.g. the American Indians? *I hereby claim all land on Earth.* Is it ethical for me to now steal back all the land that the world stole from me? And what would you say if a Seminole tribe knocked on your door one day, demanding its land back?

With that in mind, are there any enduring standards of morality? And, if not, do you have the right to arrogantly impose your ethics on other people? Is it okay for you to judge someone based on their view of abortion, for example?

Learning and Wisdom

The above are just a few examples designed to make you question.

Learn to doubt. Everything. Your parents' views, your friends' views, your own views. Where did those views come from? Were they the result of many days' research, consideration, and thought, or rather a gut feeling?

The early teen years are awkward because so many questions spring up at once. The way each person answers those questions determines her or his identity. The surer she is of her answers, the more secure her identity. Elderly people are often struck with a sense of *wisdom*: you can't teach an old dog new tricks. But don't be fooled. A person who has *decided* on his beliefs has given up learning, and a person who gives up learning is already dead. My identity changes by the moment because I learn by the moment.

Beware of quick, flowing, pat answers. A million zillion answers exist. Some of them spread better than others, for whatever reason. An answer that is capable of infecting a mind, reproducing, and then spreading is going to become a commonly heard answer. Those who are infected with such an answer will firmly believe it. The stronger the memes, the stronger the belief.

Christianity is a collection of memes that has been successful in infecting, reproducing, and spreading. Politicians, preachers, and the press thrive on successful memes. These memes do not necessarily represent truth. They simply represent what is most interesting, scary, desirable, and attention-getting.

On the first printing of *At Least in Hell the Christians Won't Harass Me*, I have no way of knowing how successful its memes are. This philosophy may be squashed like an armadillo on the information super-highway and later be re-invented by individual geniuses of the future who arrogantly believe they've come upon something new[2].

I'm hoping for good memes. I've done my best. I gave it a bright, red cover, with the word *HELL* large and bold. Inside the book, I said a lot of things to make the Christians mad and the freethinkers rejoice. I asked a lot of interesting, time-enduring questions. I designed it to irk some emotions. Ultimately, I gave it the best memes I could in an attempt to sell it. If this philosophy ever becomes the *In Thing*, I'll be way hip with the chicks. They might call me the King of Truth. I might even get a cover on *Playgirl*.

But beware of what irks your emotions. Because this book has a purpose, too. And if you doubt my message, then my purpose has been served.

If you believe that there are possibilities I haven't considered or evidence that I am not aware of, I am awake and listening. Just send a letter to me at the address printed on the copyright page if you've got an improvement or a healthy addition to this philosophy. A quote from the Bible is *not* evidence of anything, though, so don't put me on your *to-save-from-the-pits-of-Hell* mailing list. Clear, logical reasoning and constructive corrections will receive my immediate, undivided

---

[2]I get the irony, so don't bother mentioning it.

attention.

Purpose in Life (and Afterlife)

What should I do with my life? The only thing I will ultimately own is my consciousness and the memories within. A *No Fear* T-shirt popular in the early 90's read, "The one who dies with the most toys still dies." No matter how hard you work, the fruits of your labor will last no longer than your body will. Sam Walton died a few years ago, his net worth estimated at over twenty billion dollars. I can only hope that his wealth accidentally sprung from a life of many valuable experiences and dreams pursued because, if not, he took with him none of his wealth when he died.

Pleasure and pain are absolute sensations that are determined by the moment, and *only* the moment. If one's only mission is to experience pleasure, then his goal for time T in the future is to experience pleasure at T. But once T has passed, the pleasure experienced at T is done and gone. It has no effect on future absolute sensations. So the initial goal, itself, was senseless.

Say, for example, that a person had to burn every dollar he received at the moment he received it. Would making money be a wise or sensible goal? No. Similarly, neither is pursuing pleasure by itself.

The only thing I can pursue that will ultimately remain my possession is knowledge, in the form of experiences and sensations.

That's my answer to the burning question, *What should I do with my life?* Learn. Live. Experience. That's all. *And what should I do for eternity?* Learn.

Live. And experience.

Even though pleasure, itself, is a senseless goal, it does make sense to pursue experiences that are pleasurable. If you do, then at any given time, it is more likely that you are experiencing pleasure than pain. And the resulting pleasurable experiences will be yours forever.

If there are no absolute standards of morality, and I suspect that this is the case, then it really doesn't matter *what* you do. There is nothing *evil* about any particular pleasurable experience. Smoke a joint. Have lots of sex with lots of people. Gamble your life away. Just keep in mind that lots of experiences that feel good now may have painful repercussions in the future. With that aside, I believe that the worldly man is much richer than the one who lives a sheltered life of ignorance.

Welcome to Eternity

Don't spend your life getting into Heaven. There is no Heaven. And don't shelter yourself from the evils of Hell; experience all facets of living.

You'll love, learn, work, and play forever. You'll hurt, cry, rejoice, and dance forever.

But don't take it for granted. You've got now.

Live now.

You'll never get a second chance to live this moment.

Appendix A
Logic Refresher

Logic is the basis of common sense. It is what allows us to make rational conclusions based on propositions that we believe to be true. Within the realm of logic is the ability to devise rational arguments with valid conclusions. This refresher will only touch on some of the logic utilized in this book.

Logical Arguments

There are many methods for proving something. One way is proof by contradiction. Here, one simply disproves a statement, thereby proving the opposite of the statement.

(i) Assume: x (some statement).
(ii) Statement (i) is false.
(iii) Therefore, x' is true[1].

Here's an example.

(i) Assume: I am green.
(ii) Statement (i) is false.
(iii) Therefore, I am not green.

A broader method of proving something is by listing all mutually exclusive possibilities and disproving all but one. The one that remains must necessarily be the truth. Mutual exclusivity means that if a statement is true, then no mutually exclusive statement can be true. Here's an example.

(i) Either w, x, y, or z must be true. (Only one can be true.)
(ii) w is false.
(iii) x is false.
(iv) y is false.
(v) Therefore, z is true.

Here's another example.

(i) k mod 4 must equal 0, 1, 2, or 3, where k is some integer.
(ii) By (i), 125 mod 4 must equal 0, 1, 2, or 3.

---

[1]x' means *not x*, or the opposite of x. If x is "I am green," then x' is "I am not green."

(iii) 125 mod 4 does not equal 0.
(iv) 125 mod 4 does not equal 2.
(v) 125 mod 4 does not equal 3.
(vi) Therefore, 125 mod 4 equals 1.

Logic uses other proof methods, but I'll use these two almost exclusively in providing arguments for the answering of questions.

Statement Equivalences

The contrapositive of a statement is equivalent to that statement. In other words, if a statement is true, then its contrapositive is true--e.g. if a statement is false, then its contrapositive is false. A contrapositive manipulates an if-then statement as follows. Statement: "If x, then y." Contrapositive: "If not y, then not x."

The inverse and converse of a statement have a different form, but they are equivalent to each other. Consider the statement, "If x, then y." The inverse would be, "If not x, then not y," and the converse would be "If y, then x." Notice that the inverse and the converse are equivalent because the inverse is the *contrapositive* of the converse! Let me clarify these sentence forms with the following example.

Statement: If Ralph is Christian, then Ralph believes in God.

Inverse: If Ralph is not Christian, then Ralph does not believe in God.

Converse: If Ralph believes in God, then Ralph is Christian.

Contrapositive: If Ralph does not believe in God, then Ralph is not a Christian.

Only the statement and its contrapositive are necessarily true. A Jew believes in God, but a Jew is not Christian. Similarly, a Jew is not a Christian, but a Jew does believe in God.

If a statement and its converse (or inverse) are true, then the statement is said to imply its converse, and vice verse.

(i) If x, then y.
(ii) If y, then x.
(iii) So, x if and only if y—also written as "x iff y."
(iv) Clearly, y if and only if x, too.

Here is an example.

(i) If my name is Andrew Knight and I am a graduate student at the University of Florida, then I am the author of this book. (True.)
(ii) If I am the author of this book, then my name is Andrew Knight and I am a graduate student at the University of Florida. (True.)
(iii) So, my name is Andrew Knight and I am a graduate student at the University of Florida *if and only if* I am the author of this book.

Exercises

Mutual Exclusivity

Problem #1: What is the most appropriate conclusion for statement (iv)?
(i) x and y are the only mutually exclusive possibilities.
(ii) If x, then z.
(iii) If y, then z.
(iv) So...

Statement Equivalences

Problem #2: What's wrong with this proof?
(i) An apple is a fruit.
(ii) An orange is a fruit.
(iii) So, an apple is an orange.

Invalid Arguments

Problem #3: Although the evaluation of the validity of a logical argument is beyond the scope of this book, I include the following problem as a mental challenge to advanced readers.

In the first printing of this book[1], I used the following "proof" to show statement (IX)[2]. Show how the following argument is flawed—i.e. why I had to implement a different proof in this book.

> For any given point in time T_1, only the two following mutually exclusive possibilities exist.
>
> (A) I will recall T_1 at one or more points in the future.
> (B) I will never recall T_1.
>
> Consider statement (A). Two more mutually exclusive possibilities exist.
>
> (a) If at some point T_2 in the future I will recall some point T_1 in the past, then I was unconscious at point T_1.
> (b) If at some point T_2 in the future I will recall some point T_1 in the past, then I was conscious at point T_1.
>
> Assume (a) to be correct. Then the contrapositive must be correct.

[1]*Absolute Truth*, ISBN 0-9661026-0-6.

[2]I am conscious during an event if and only if I will recall the event. I am unconscious during an event if and only if I will never recall the event.

(i) If at some point T_2 in the future I will recall some point T_1 in the past, then I was unconscious at point T_1.
(ii) Contrapositive: if I was conscious at point T_1 in the past, then at no point in the future will I recall point T_1.
(iii) I recall points in the past when I was conscious.
(iv) Contradiction. Thus, statement (a) is false.
(v) So, statement (b) is true.
(vi) Also, the contrapositive of (b) is true: if I was unconscious at point T_1 in the past, then at no point in the future will I recall point T_1.

Consider statement (B). Two more mutually exclusive possibilities exist.

(c) If I will never recall point T_1 in the past, then I was conscious at T_1.
(d) If I will never recall point T_1 in the past, then I was unconscious at T_1.

Assume (c) to be correct.

(i) If I will never recall point T_1 in the past, then I was conscious at T_1.
(ii) Statement (b) is true. (If at some point T_2 in the future I will recall some point T_1 in the past, then I was conscious at point T_1.)

(iii) Since (b) and (c) represent two mutually exclusive possibilities, then I must necessarily be conscious at T_1, because this is the conclusion of both statements.
(iv) I am not always conscious.
(v) Contradiction. Thus, statement (c) is false.
(vi) So, statement (d) is true.
(vii) Also, the contrapositive of (d) is true: if I was conscious at point T_1 in the past, then I will at some point in the future recall T_1.

Combining statements (b) and (d), which are inverses of each other, we arrive at the following.

(IX) I am conscious during an event if and only if I will recall the event. I am unconscious during an event if and only if I will never recall the event.

Solutions

Answer #1: (iv) So, z.

It should make sense that if only two mutually exclusive possibilities exist, and they both come to the same conclusion, then that conclusion must be the only possibility—and therefore correct. This is called *disjunctive syllogism*.

Answer #2: The verb *is* classifies. To say that *water is a liquid* is to say that *water is a type of liquid*. And to say that *Leroy is a Neanderthal* is to say that *Leroy is one of the Neanderthal type*. *If* a thing is member of a classification, *then* it is of that type. So, *water is a liquid* implies *if water, then a liquid*. And *Leroy is a Neanderthal* implies *if Leroy, then a Neanderthal*. The proof in Problem #2 is corrected here.

(i) An apple is a fruit.
(ii) So, if an apple, then a fruit.
(iii) A statement is not necessarily equivalent to its converse.
(iv) If a fruit, then not necessarily an apple.
(v) An orange is a fruit.
(vi) An orange is not necessarily an apple.

Answer #3: The first mistake is statement (iii) when considering statement (A). Although it is true—I *do* recall some points in the past when I was conscious—and although all statements preceding it are true, (iii) does *not* contradict (ii). Statement (ii) refers to a specific T_1 and may not be true for all times. So, just because I recall points in the past says nothing about whether I recall T_1.

However, this is not the vital mistake. Although it is true that this mistake completely invalidates its conclusion, the conclusion does not even require a proof! We take it on common sense that recalling T_1 requires that one is conscious at T_1. This simple and agreeable statement is (IV) in this book.

The vital mistake is a similar one: statement (iv) when considering statement (B) does not contradict statement (iii). Again, both statements are true, but the fact that I was conscious at T_1 (the claim of statement (iii)) says nothing about my consciousness at other times.

Appendix B
Calculus and Statistics Refresher

This appendix is designed to review basic concepts in calculus and statistics which are necessary to understand and apply the mathematical model introduced in *What is Déjà Vu?*

Calculus

Function

A function maps one value to another. A two-dimensional function maps an independent variable to the other variable, which is necessarily dependent.

For example, the phrase *sensation function* was

defined in this book as a function which maps some stimulus to a resulting sensation. An absolute sensation function is a function that maps some stimulus to a resulting absolute sensation. Since stimuli are time-dependent, then an absolute sensation function can also be written as a function of time. This (time-dependent) function was modeled as a decaying exponential function, which, like any mathematical model, may not be perfectly accurate. Most functions utilized in this book are time-dependent, which means that they are two-dimensional and depend on time, which is an independent variable. Even though these are relatively simple functions to work with, their derivatives and integrals are necessary to model the relationship between stimulus, position, and absolute sensation.

Derivative

The slope of a function at some point is calculated by its derivative at that point. In high school algebra, the slope of a line is calculated as *rise over run*. A line can be drawn between any two points, and the slope of that line is the quotient of the *change in y* to the *change in x*, where y is a function of x. So the slope of a function at some point can be approximated by choosing two more points (one on either side of the first point) and determining the slope between those two points. As those two points get closer and closer to the first point, their slope better approximates the slope of the function at that point.

Let (x,y) be some point on a function. Let (x_1,y_1)

be some point before (x,y) and (x_2,y_2) be some point after (x,y). Then the *derivative* at (x,y) is defined as the slope of the function at (x,y), which is calculated by the following.

$$\lim_{\substack{x_1 \to x \\ x_2 \to x}} \frac{(y_2-y_1)}{(x_2-x_1)}$$

Instead of having two points approach the point in question, only one additional point is needed. If we are trying to find the derivative of a function at (x,y), where y = f(x), then we can choose some point $[x+\Delta x, f(x+\Delta x)]$ and find the slope between these two points. The derivative is calculated by allowing $[x+\Delta x, f(x+\Delta x)]$ to approach [x,f(x)], by letting Δx (and its corresponding Δy) to approach zero.

$$f'(x) = \lim_{\Delta x \to 0} \frac{f(x+\Delta x) - f(x)}{(x+\Delta x - x)}$$

$$= \lim_{\Delta x \to 0} \frac{f(x+\Delta x) - f(x)}{\Delta x}, \qquad (1)$$

which is the accepted form for a derivative.

If y (or f) is dependent on only one variable, say x, then the first derivative of y is written y'(x), the second is written y''(x), and so forth. If y is dependent on more than one variable, then partial derivatives are necessary.

Partial derivatives will not be covered here because they are not required for your comprehension of the models in this book. If y is dependent on a dependent variable, then the derivative of y must specify which variable it is calculated with respect to. Say, for example, that y is dependent on x, but x is dependent on t. Then y is also dependent on t, but the derivative of y with respect to x will be different than the derivative of y with respect to t. In this case, the derivative must be specified as dy/dx or dy/dt[1].

Here is an example. If $f(x) = 3x^2$, then what is $f'(x)$ at any point?

$$f'(x) = \lim_{\Delta x \to 0} \frac{f(x+\Delta x) - f(x)}{\Delta x}$$

$$= \lim_{\Delta x \to 0} \frac{3(x+\Delta x)^2 - 3x^2}{\Delta x}$$ (substitution of f(x))

$$= \lim_{\Delta x \to 0} \frac{3(x^2+2x\Delta x+\Delta x^2) - 3x^2}{\Delta x}$$ (expansion of $(x+\Delta x)^2$)

$$= \lim_{\Delta x \to 0} \frac{3x^2 + 6x\Delta x + 3\Delta x^2 - 3x^2}{\Delta x}$$ (distribution of 3)

---

[1]The form dy/dt, for example, simply means the infinitesimal change in y divided by the corresponding infinitesimal change in t, which is exactly the same as the derivative of y with respect to t.

$$= \lim_{\Delta x \to 0} \frac{6x\Delta x + 3\Delta x^2}{\Delta x}$$ (cancellation of $3x^2$)

$$= \lim_{\Delta x \to 0} 6x + 3\Delta x$$ (division by Δx)

$= 6x + 0 = 6x.$ (evaluation of limit)

You don't need to calculate all derivatives from scratch, since mathematicians did the dirty work for us many years ago. You can look in any calculus book for a chart of derivatives, but I will print here the only ones you will need for the functions in this book.

$(c)' = 0;$ (2)

$[g(x) + h(x)]' = g'(x) + h'(x);$ (3)

$\{c[g(x)]\}' = c[g'(x)];$ (4)

$[c(e^{ax})]' = ac(e^{ax});$ (5)

$\{c[\ln(ax)]\}' = c/x;$ (6)

$(x^a)' = ax^{a-1},$ (7)

where a and c are Real constants.

Integral

If one knows f '(x), then f(x) can be calculated and is called an antiderivative of f '(x). Actually, there are an infinite number of antiderivatives for any function f '(x), and here's why.

$$f'(x) = f'(x) + 0.$$

$$\text{Antiderivative of } f'(x) = (\text{ad}^2 \text{ of } f'(x)) + (\text{ad of } 0)$$
$$= f(x) + c, \qquad (8)$$

where c is some constant and is called a *constant of integration*. Let's double check our math.

$$(f(x) + c)' = f'(x) + (c)' = f'(x) + 0 = f'(x).$$

The antiderivative of a function is called an indefinite integral. The constant c can only be calculated with initial conditions. Let's try another example. What is the indefinite integral of $f(x) = 4e^{6x}$? In other words, name some function F(x) such that F'(x) = f(x). By guessing and checking, we find that $F(x) = (2/3)e^{6x} + c$, since

$$F'(x) = 6(2/3)e^{6x} + 0 = 4e^{6x} = f(x).$$

What is c if F(0) = 0?

[2]Antiderivative

$F(0) = 0 = (2/3)e^0 + c$ (evaluation at x=0)

$= (2/3) + c.$ (evaluation of e^0)

Solving for c,

$c = -(2/3).$

Thus, the final indefinite integral is $F(x) = (2/3)(e^{6x}) - (2/3)$. But what exactly is the use of an integral? The derivative of a function is useful because it tells us the slope of that function (at some point). But what does the integral tell us? First, let's look at its characteristics.

(a.1) Whenever a function is increasing, its derivative is positive.
(a.2) Whenever a function is positive, its integral is increasing.
(b.1) Whenever a function is decreasing, its derivative is negative.
(b.2) Whenever a function is negative, its integral is decreasing.
(c.1) Whenever a function is remaining constant (neither increasing nor decreasing), its derivative is zero.
(c.2) Whenever a function is zero, its integral is remaining constant.

If you let these facts kind of roll around in your head, it will eventually occur to you that the integral of a function tells approximately how much area the function has enclosed. Whenever the function is positive, there is a positive area under the function, so the integral increases. And whenever the function is negative, there is *negative* area above the function, so the integral decreases.

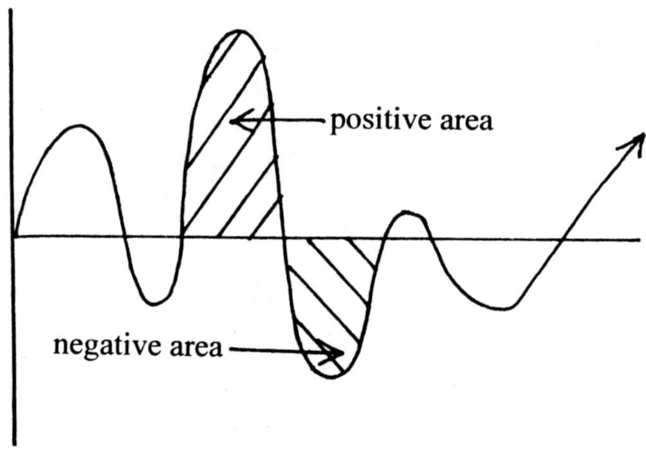

A definite integral is the amount of area that has been mapped out by a function between two points. It is calculated by the sum of all areas mapped by f(x)dx[3] as follows.

[3]The notation f(x)dx is necessary in evaluating the integral of f(x). f(x) is a single dimension, and in order to calculate the area mapped by f(x) on the x-axis, f(x) must be multiplied by another dimension, dx. Don't forget that area is a two-dimensional value.

$$\int_{x_1}^{x_2} f(x)dx$$

$= [F(x) + c]$ evaluated between x_1 and x_2

$$= [F(x) + c]_{x_2}^{x_1} = F(x_2) + c - (F(x_1) + c)$$

$$= F(x_2) - F(x_1) + c - c = F(x_2) - F(x_1), \tag{9}$$

where F(x) is an antiderivative of f(x).

Again, you can find a table of integrals in any calculus book, but the ones that will be utilized in this book are the following.

$$\int 0dx = c; \tag{10}$$

$$\int [g(x) + h(x)]dx = \int g(x)dx + \int h(x)dx; \tag{11}$$

$$\int a(f(x))dx = a \int f(x)dx; \tag{12}$$

$$\int e^{ax}dx = e^{ax}/a + c; \tag{13}$$

$$\int (a/x)dx = a(\ln(x)) + c; \tag{14}$$

$$\int x^{a}dx = x^{a+1}/(a+1) + c, \tag{15}$$

where a is a constant and c is some constant of integration.

Just as a function can have a first, second, and third derivative ad infinitum, a function can also have a single, double, and triple integral ad infinitum. A single integral maps out area (2-D), a double integral maps out volume (3-D), a triple integral maps out space (4-D), and who knows what a quadruple or quintuple integral maps out! Luckily, multiple integrations, as well as integrals with respect to dependent variables, are not utilized in this book.

Differential Equations

Back in the fourth grade, all of the answers to your math problems were numbers. If $3x + 5 = 14$, then $x = 3$. But in advanced mathematics, the solutions to problems are often equations, not numbers at all. For example, if $y'(x) = 4x^3 + 1/x$, then one solution to this differential equation would be $y(x) = x^4 + \ln(x) - 7$. But what about $y''(x) - 4y(x) = f(x)$[4]? This can be rewritten as $(D^2 - 4)y(x) = f(x)$. Here, $D^2 - 4$ is called the *indicial equation* of this differential equation.

[4]f(x) is some arbitrary function which could be zero.

Without showing you the derivation, it turns out that there are exactly two orthogonal[5] solutions to the homogeneous equation (where f(x) = 0) of the above differential equation, written of this form:

$$y_1(x) = \exp(D_1 x), \quad (16)$$
$$y_2(x) = \exp(D_2 x), \quad (17)$$

where D_1 and D_2 are the roots to the indicial equation. Here, D = 2 or -2. The general solution to the homogeneous equation is

$$y_h(x) = c_1(y_1(x)) + c_2(y_2(x)), \quad (18)$$

where c_1 and c_2 are arbitrary constants. But what about the original equation, where f(x) is not zero? You must find some *particular* solution to the equation, $y_p(x)$, and when you do, the general solution to the original differential equation is

$$y_g(x) = y_h(x) + y_p(x). \quad (19)$$

A particular solution is often very difficult to obtain. Sometimes you can figure it out just by staring at the differential equation, sometimes you have to guess

---

[5]For the sake of simplicity, a function cannot be represented as a linear combination of *orthogonal* functions. For example, x, x^2, and x^3 are orthogonal because there is no way to get x from a linear combination of x^2 and x^3.

and check, and sometimes you have to implement powerful computers to engage complex algorithms to find a particular solution. You will not have to find any particular solutions to differential equations in this book.

The above example explained how to solve a second order differential equation. A first-order differential equation, those utilized in this book, are solved almost identically. The only difference is that the indicial equation of a first-order differential equation is linear, which is easy to solve and always has a real root[6].

$$Ay'(x) + By(x) = f(x) \rightarrow (AD + B)y(x) = f(x).$$

The indicial equation to this differential equation is $AD + B = 0$, so $D = -(B/A)$. The homogeneous solution is

$$y_h(x) = c(e^{-(B/A)x}), \quad (20)$$

where c is some constant. To find the general solution, you must first find some particular solution $y_p(x)$ which depends on $f(x)$. $y_p(x) = 0$ if $f(x) = 0$. The general solution is then of this form.

$$y_g(x) = c(e^{-(B/A)x}) + y_p(x). \quad (21)$$

---

[6]Quadratic indicial equations have two roots which are both Real or both Imaginary. An nth order indicial equation will have exactly n roots, which may not all be Real.

Statistics

What is the expected probability that a tossed coin will produce heads? 50%. So, if you flip a coin twice, does that mean that exactly 50% of those tosses will be heads? Is it possible to flip two tails or two heads? Of course. Is it likely? Yes. Is it possible to flip one million consecutive tails or one million consecutive heads? Of course. Is it likely? Not very. If is far more likely that a meteorite kills you right now. It is also more likely that you make contact with an intelligent alien society.

So if you flip a coin ten times, what percentage of the tosses will be heads? Anywhere from 0% to 100%. What about if you flipped a coin a hundred times? It will *probably* range from 25% to 75%. What about a thousand tosses? It will *probably* range from 45% to 55%. What about a million tosses? It will *probably* range from 49.9% to 50.1%. In other words, as the number of tosses approaches infinity, the expected fraction of heads (or tails) approaches 50%. Here we introduce the bell curve, also known as a z-distribution. Let the number of coin tosses here be small (like 20).

(See next page for distribution plot.)

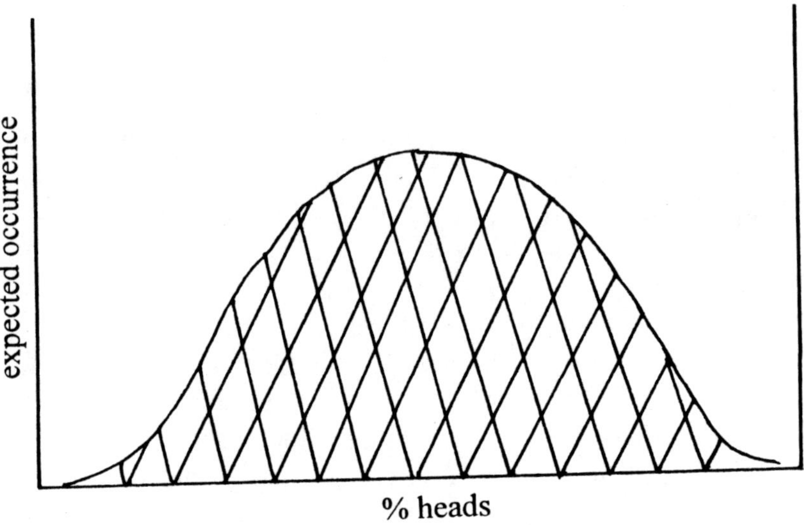

There is a 100% chance that the percentage of heads will range from 0% to 100%, so the sum of all possibilities must equal 100%. Therefore the integral of any bell curve must exactly converge to 100% (or 1).

With a small number of coin tosses (n-value), it is hard to say whether or not the percentage of heads will be near 50%, so the bell curve corresponding to this *n* will be wide, where n is the number of tosses. As n increases, the curve becomes thinner and thinner, meaning that it is more likely to find the correct percentage of heads closer to 50%. As n approaches infinity, the probability of 50% heads approaches one, and everything else approaches zero. In this last graph, let the number of coin tosses be very large, like a million.

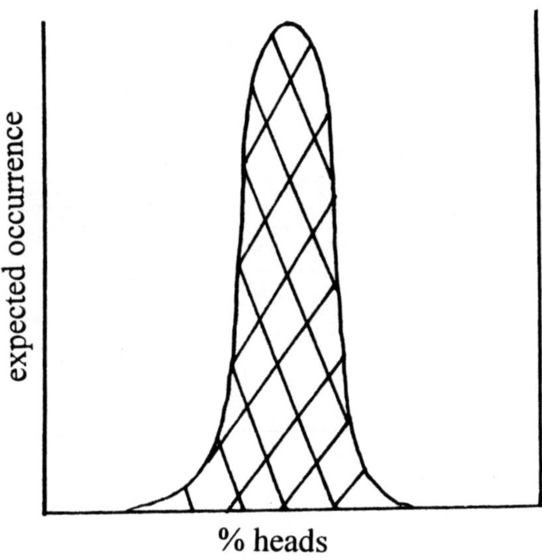

In *Is There an End to Eternity?*, simple statistics are necessary to understand the probabilistic nature of memory modifications and absolute sensations. In the case of memory modifications, as time progresses, the height to the 95% probability limit narrows, in much the same way that the above z-distribution narrows as the number of coin tosses increases. This probability limit will continue to narrow to zero as time approaches infinity.

Exercises

Derivative

Problem #1: Derive the first derivative of $f(x) = x^n$ using only the definition of derivative.

Problem #2: Evaluate the first derivative of the following functions.

(a) $f(x) = (1/4)x^4 + x^3 + 18$.

(b) $f(x) = 3\ln(8x)$.

(c) $f(x) = 2e^{-5x} + x + 1$.

Integral

Problem #3: $f(x) = 3x^2 + 2$.

(a) Find an antiderivative of f(x).

(b) Find the indefinite integral of f(x) where F(0) = 5.

(c) Find the definite integral of f(x) from 0 to 4.

Differential Equation

Problem #4: Solve the following second-order differential equation.

$4y''(x) - 36y(x) = -40\sin(x)$.

Verify that the particular solution to this differential equation is $y_p(x) = \sin(x)$.

Solutions

Answer #1:

$$\lim_{\Delta x \to 0} \frac{f(x+\Delta x) - f(x)}{\Delta x}$$

$$= \lim_{\Delta x \to 0} \frac{(x+\Delta x)^n - x^n}{\Delta x}$$ (evaluation of function)

$$= \lim_{\Delta x \to 0} \frac{\{x^n + n(x^{n-1})\Delta x + c_1(x^{n-2})\Delta x^2 + c_2(x^{n-3})\Delta x^3 + \ldots}{\Delta x}$$

$$\frac{+ c_{n-2}(x)\Delta x^{n-1} + c_{n-1}(\Delta x^n)\} - x^n}{\Delta x},$$

(polynomial expansion)

where c_1, c_2, ..., c_{n-1} are the coefficients of polynomial expansion,

$$= \lim_{\Delta x \to 0} \frac{n(x^{n-1})\Delta x + c_1(x^{n-2})\Delta x^2 + \ldots + c_{n-1}(\Delta x^n)}{\Delta x}$$

(cancellation of x^n)

$$= \lim_{\Delta x \to 0} n(x^{n-1}) + c_1(x^{n-2})\Delta x + \ldots + c_{n-1}(\Delta x^{n-1})$$

(division by Δx)

$= n(x^{n-1}) + 0 + 0 + \ldots = n(x^{n-1})$. (evaluation of limit)

Answer #2:

(a) $f'(x) = [(1/4)x^4]' + [x^3]' + [18]'$
$= 4(1/4)x^{4-1} + 3x^{3-1} + 0$
$= x^3 + 3x^2$.

(b) $f'(x) = 3/x$.

(c) $f'(x) = [2e^{-5x}]' + [x]' + [1]'$
$= -5(2e^{-5x}) + 1x^{1-1} + 0$
$= -10e^{-5x} + 1$.

Answer #3:

(a) $F(x) = x^3 + 2x + c$, where c is an arbitrary constant.

(b) $F(0) = 5 = (0)^3 + 2(0) + c$, so $c = 5$. $F(x) = x^3 + 2x + 5$.

(c) $$\int_0^4 f(x)dx = F(4) - F(0) = 77 - 5 = 72.$$

Answer #4: The indicial equation is $D^2 - 9 = 0$, so $D = \{3,-3\}$. The homogeneous solution is

$$y_h(x) = c_1 e^{3x} + c_2 e^{-3x},$$

where c_1 and c_2 are real constants. $y_p(x) = \sin(x)$ is a particular solution to the differential equation because

$$4y_p''(x) - 36y_p(x)$$

$$= 4(\sin(x))'' - 36\sin(x)$$

$$= -4\sin(x) - 36\sin(x) = -40\sin(x).$$

So, a general solution is of the form

$$y_g(x) = y_p(x) + y_h(x) = \sin(x) + c_1 e^{3x} + c_2 e^{-3x}.$$

The Author

Courtesy of David Blankenship

Andrew Knight is a nuclear engineering graduate student at the University of Florida. He currently resides in Gainesville.